CW01065082

SOUTH SHIELDS F.C.
The Football League Years

By George Thompson

Published by:
Yore Publications
12 The Furrows, Harefield,
Middx. UB9 6AT.

© George Thompson 2000

....

All rights reserved.
No part of this publication may be reproduced
or copied in any manner without the prior permission
in writing of the copyright holder.

British Library Cataloguing-in-Publication Data.
A catalogue record for this book
is available from the British Library.

ISBN 978-1-87442-743-8
Reprinted 2017

Printed in the UK by 4edge Limited

Dedicated

To Jenny

The best cook in Surrey

~ Acknowledgements ~

Thanks are due to many people for the help I have received in recording the progress and decline of South Shields Football Club. The project would not have been possible without the many authors of books on football clubs whose research must have seemed never ending. In turn much of that research was assisted by that patron saint of football history, Jim Creasy, whom I have had the pleasure of meeting on a number of occasions. The staff of various libraries and archives deserve my thanks as well, particularly the ever-cheerful and helpful ladies and gentlemen at the Newspaper Library Colindale who have trundled many a barrow laden with volumes of the 'Sunday Sun', 'Shields Gazette' and 'Northern Echo', on my behalf.

Thanks to Robert F. Wray of Cleadon Village, especially for the loan of very valuable photographs from his collection. Mr Robert Gate, the distinguished historian of Rugby League kindly answered a query concerning Jack Tinn's early connection with that sport. Barry Le Boutillier, no football fan but genealogist par excellence, made a valuable suggestion which led to the discovery of early information.

In presenting my manuscript (and making it legible), thanks are due to Alan Carter, Fred Dowry and to Dave Twydell's daughter Kara - the world's leading expert in the presentation of tabulated football facts and figures. And of course to Dave himself, another patron saint of football history, for publishing this work.

Thanks to you all.

George Thompson
May 2000.

Contents

North Eastern League Days 1908-1915

SOUTH SHIELDS ADELAIDE A.F.C
1908-9.

Although there had been a senior football club in South Shields from 1897 it seems to have had a short life and to have fallen foul of the local football authorities. South Shields Adelaide were founded in 1904 and played in the Tyneside League winning the championship at the first attempt.

Professional football in the town began when South Shields Adelaide joined the North Eastern League in 1908. A brief note of the history of this League would be in order. It had been instigated by Newcastle United who were dissatisfied with the opposition faced by their reserve or 'A' team in the Northern League. It was felt that a League comprised mostly of the reserve sides of Football League clubs would present a more appropriate challenge to aspiring First Division players. An inaugural meeting was held in the St. James' Park boardroom in May 1906, attended by representatives of the three major North Eastern clubs as well as Bradford City, Hull City and Leeds City. Originally it was hoped that the reserve sides of other Yorkshire clubs would join.

Also invited were a number of non-League clubs, and when the North Eastern League began operating in September, Hebburn Argyle, Sunderland Royal Rovers and West Stanley joined the reserve sides of Newcastle United, Sunderland, Middlesbrough, Leeds City, Bradford

City, Carlisle United and Workington. It should be stressed that the last named pair fielded their first teams in the Lancashire Combination.

Interestingly, the initial North Eastern League champions - Newcastle United Reserves - were presented with the Oxo Trophy. This was clearly an early football sponsorship by a company trying to steal a march on its rival (Bovril) which was advertised and sold at football grounds everywhere, the products of both companies were always welcome on cold Saturday afternoons.

When South Shields Adelaide joined the North Eastern League in 1908 the only remaining Yorkshire reserve side was that of Bradford (Park Avenue). The first teams of newly formed Huddersfield Town and Hartlepools United joined at the same time.

Although North Eastern League games were reported extensively in newspapers and sometimes drew five figure crowds, Newcastle United wearied of their brainchild and left for the more appropriate Central League in 1933. Sunderland and Middles-brough's reserve sides had to be content with much inferior opponents for many years even after the North Eastern League ended in 1957. After 1936 one of the more prominent clubs was the later South Shields F.C.

1908/09 Season: North-Eastern League

Date	Opponent	Result	Scorers
Sep 5	HUDDERSFIELD TOWN	2-0	Atkinson, Howe
12	NORTH SHIELDS ATH.	2-0	Cassidy, Howe(pen)
26	Huddersfield Town	2-1	Hardie, Atkinson
Oct 10	HEBBURN ARGYLE	3-1	Atkinson, Ford, Howe
24	Sunderland Royal Rovers	3-1	Howe(2,1pen), Cassidy
31	SEAHAM WHITE STAR	2-1	Cassidy(2)
Dec 19	WALLSEND PARK VILLA	1-2	Hails
25	North Shields Athletic	0-1	
26	West Stanley	1-3	Hails
Jan 1	MIDDLESBROUGH RES.	2-1	Howe, Cail
2	Spennymoor United	2-4	Cassidy, Howe
9	Carlisle United Res.	6-1	Hardie, Hails(3), Cassidy(2)
16	WEST STANLEY	3-2	Hails(2), Howe
23	Shildon	4-1	Cassidy(2), Atkinson, Davies
30	NEWCASTLE UTD. RES.	0-2	
Feb 13	Hartlepools United	2-2	Hails(2)
20	Bradford Res.	3-1	Cassidy, Ford, Hails
27	SUNDERLAND RES.	1-1	Lowe
Mar 13	Seaham White Star	0-2	
17	CARLISLE UTD RES,	4-1	Hails, Cassidy, Howe(2)
24	Darlington	1-3	Cassidy
27	SUNDERLAND ROY. ROV.	4-0	Hails(3), Howe
31	Hebburn Argy,e	2-0	Hardie, Howe
Apr 3	SHILDON	3-0	Atkinson, Newton(p), Cassidy
9	Middlesbrough Res.	1-0	Howe
10	HARTLEPOOLS UNITED	1-1	Cassidy
12	SPENNYMOOR UNITED	4-0	Howe, Cassidy(2), Hails
13	WORKINGTON RES.	6-0	Davie,Hails(2),Newton(p),Howe
14	Sunderland Res.	2-0	Cassidy(2)
17	BRADFORD RES.	4-2	Cassidy(2), Howe, Hails
22	Workington Res.	3-1	Cassidy, Davie, Howe
24	Newcastle United Res.	2-0	Cassidy(2)
26	Wallsend Park Villa	0-2	

A 3,000 crowd saw South Shields Adelaide win their first professional game on a wet day in September. After winning their first six games the club then went seven weeks without playing another North Eastern League match. Many vacant Saturdays were taken up by various local and national cup-ties.

Football's internal politics reared its ugly head after the home match with Newcastle United Reserves on 30 January. A myster-ious matter concerning a cheque with which the club paid the Durham Football Assoc-iation's share of the match receipts resulted in the suspension of several of the club's officials including secretary Jack Tinn.

The backlog of fixtures meant that twelve games had to be crammed into April. The Workington Reserve side which lost 6-0 at Horsley Hill on 12 April had played two matches the previous day losing 5-0 at both Hartlepools and Seaham - South Shields Adelaide finished in second place.

A prominent North Eastern League club was West Stanley. This Durham village was the scene of a terrible mining disaster on 13 February 1909. The club trainer was one of 168 men who lost their lives that day.

1908/09 North-Eastern League

	P	W	D	L	F	A	Pts
1. Newcastle United 'A'	34	26	4	4	106	48	56
2. SOUTH SHIELDS ADELAIDE	34	22	4	8	80	41	48
3. Bradford Park Avenue 'A'	34	19	5	10	84	49	43
4. Hartlepools United	34	16	9	9	79	51	41
5. Middlesbrough 'A'	34	17	6	11	82	45	40
6. Sunderland 'A'	34	18	3	13	81	54	39
7. West Stanley	34	18	3	13	73	56	39
8. Darlington	34	15	8	11	76	73	38
9. North Shields Athletic	34	14	6	14	63	48	34
10. Spennymoor United	34	13	7	14	55	63	33
11. Wallsend Park Villa	34	13	6	15	55	66	32
12. Workington	34	12	5	17	50	80	29
13. Seaham White Star	34	10	7	17	55	64	27
14. Hebburn Argyle	34	10	6	18	55	91	26
15. Carlisle United	34	10	4	20	61	84	24
16. Huddersfield Town	34	10	4	20	47	78	24
17. Shildon Athletic	34	7	6	21	51	101	20
18. Sunderland Royal Rovers	34	7	5	22	39	100	19

1909/10 Season: North-Eastern League

Sep	4	SEAHAM HARBOUR	4-2	P.McLauchlan(3), Hall
	11	Hebburn Argyle	0-1	
	25	WINGATE ALBION	5-0	P.McLauchlan(3), Cassidy(2)
Oct	9	Sunderland Royal Rovers	2-1	Cassidy, Howe
	16	Spennymoor United	1-2	Howe
	23	HARTLEPOOLS UNITED	1-0	Atkinson
	30	Newcastle United Res.	1-5	Hall
Nov	6	SHILDON	3-1	Howe, Cassidy, Hurdman
	13	Middlesbrough Res.	0-3	
	27	NORTH SHIELDS ATH.	3-2	Hurdman, Cassidy, Oates
Dec	4	Carlisle United Res.	1-2	Smith
	18	SUNDERLAND ROYAL ROV.	5-2	King(3), Cassidy(2)
	25	Sunderland Res.	1-1	Hall(pen)
	27	WALLSEND PARK VILLA	3-5	Hall(pen), King(2)
Jan	1	NEWCASTLE UNITED RES.	3-9	Hurdman(3)
	3	North Shields Athletic	1-1	Oates
	8	WEST STANLEY	2-0	Atkinson, Hurdman
	22	Wallsend Park Villa	0-1	
Feb	12	Seaham Harbour	1-2	Howe
	19	Wingate Albion	2-2	Hardie, Cassidy
Mar	5	Hartlepools United	1-3	King
	12	MIDDLESBROUGH RES.	2-2	Howe, Hurdman
	19	West Stanley	4-1	Hurdman(3), Cassidy
	25	SUNDERLAND RES.	0-0	
	29	CARLISLE UNITED RES.	5-2	Cassidy(2),Howe Atkinson(2)
Apr	2	Workington Res.	7-1	Cassidy(2),Howe,Needham(3),Ford(p)
	9	WORKINGTON RES.	6-0	Howe(2),Ford(p),Gaudie(2),Atkinson
	13	Shildon	1-2	Smith
	16	DARLINGTON	8-1	Howe(3),Hardie(2),Atkinson,Cassidy,Ford
	23	Darlington	0-4	
	27	HEBBURN ARGYLE	2-0	Cassidy(2)

This season was less successful with the club finishing eighth. Crowds averaged 4,000.

Patrick McLauchlan who scored hat tricks in the first and third matches left immediately for higher things but his Football League career only consisted of two appearances and one goal for Fulham

The North Eastern League championship was decided on Wednesday 27 April, when Newcastle United Reserves lost 2-0 at Hartlepools. However, the true Newcastle Reserves were all far away losing a First Division game 4-0 at Villa Park, while the first team were sunning themselves at Southport in preparation for the F.A.Cup Final replay; the team that Hartlepools United beat were in reality Newcastle United Reserves' Reserves!

1909/10 North-Eastern League	P	W	D	L	F	A	Pts
1. Spennymoor United	32	24	3	5	75	39	51
2. Newcastle United 'A'	32	21	6	5	134	31	48
3. Middlesbrough 'A'	32	21	5	6	90	51	47
4. Hartlepools United	32	18	10	4	82	23	46
5. Darlington	32	16	5	11	60	55	37
6. Sunderland 'A'	32	15	6	11	65	43	36
7. Shildon Athletic	32	13	8	11	61	61	34
8. SOUTH SHIELDS ADELAIDE	32	14	5	13	77	63	33
9. North Shields Athletic	32	12	8	12	60	61	32
10.Seaham Harbour	32	14	3	15	56	57	31
11.Wallsend Park Villa	32	12	6	14	56	67	30
12.Carlisle United Reserves	32	11	4	17	52	62	26
13.Wingate Albion	32	8	8	16	43	80	24
14.West Stanley	32	9	5	18	56	85	23
15.Hebburn Argyle	32	8	4	20	33	103	20
16.Workington Reserves	32	7	4	21	41	98	18
17.Sunderland Royal Rovers	32	2	5	25	25	83	11

1910/11 Season: North-Eastern League

Sep	3	NORTH SHIELDS ATHLETIC	0-1
	7	Sunderland Res.	2-3 Hall(2)
	10	Hebburn Argyle	1-0 Hall(pen)
	24	WINGATE ALBION	1-0 McIlvenny
Oct	8	West Stanley	0-1
	22	DARLINGTON	2-0 Johnson(2)
	29	Middlesbrough Res.	1-3 Bruce
Nov	5	CARLISLE UNITED	3-0 McIlvenny(2), Halls
	12	Spennymoor United	1-0 Oates
	19	Sunderland Royal Rovers	3-1 C.Burrell,Cassidy,McIlvenny
	26	WEST STANLEY	3-0 McIlvenny(2, Chrisp
Dec	3	NEWCASTLE UNITED RES.	1-1 McIlvenny
	10	Shildon	3-1 Chrisp, C.Burrell, McIlvenny
	24	Hartlepools United	1-1 Hall
	26	North Shields Athletic	2-0 G.Burrell, Hall
	31	SEAHAM HARBOUR	5-1 Cassidy, Hall(3), McIlvenny
Jan	2	HEBBURN ARGYLE	6-1 C.Burrell(4), Pearson, Wilson
	7	Darlington	1-2 G.Burrell
	28	SHILDON	2-0 McIlvenny, Hails
Feb	11	SUNDERLAND ROYAL ROV.	1-0 Wilson(pen)
	18	MIDDLESBROUGH RES.	2-0 G.Burrell, Hails
	25	Wallsend Park Villa	1-1 Wilson(pen)
Mar	4	Wingate Albion	1-4 Johnson
	11	Seaham Harbour	0-0
	18	Workington Res.	1-0 Johnson(pen)
	25	WALLSEND PARK VILLA	4-1 Cassidy,McCleary,Hails,G.Burrell
Apr	8	SUNDERLAND RES.	0-1
	14	WORKINGTON RES.	5-1 McCleary(4), Pringle
	15	Carlisle United	1-1 McCleary
	17	HARTLEPOOLS UNITED	1-0 McCleary
	18	Jarrow Croft	1-3 ?
	24	NEWCASTLE UTD RES.	0-3
	26	JARROW CROFT	0-1

South Shields (who had now dropped the 'Adelaide' suffix) did not play the full complement of fixtures this season. Spennymoor United were suspended late in the season and could not play the match scheduled at Horsley Hill.

High scoring Peter Cassidy transferred to First Division Bradford City late in the season but after an unimpressive campaign there he ended his career in the Southern League with Cardiff City.

From this season onwards Carlisle United's first team competed in the North Eastern League.

In the summer of 1911 South Shields' officials attended a meeting at Sheffield to discuss a proposed Third Division of the Football League.

1910/11 North-Eastern League

	P	W	D	L	F	A	Pts
1. Newcastle United 'A'	34	25	4	5	88	25	54
2. Sunderland	34	20	6	8	81	38	46
3. Hartlepools United	34	18	8	8	71	40	44
4. Darlington	34	19	5	10	79	39	43
5. **SOUTH SHIELDS**	**33**	**18**	**5**	**10**	**56**	**33**	**41**
6. North Shields Athletic	34	19	3	12	57	56	41
7. Middlesbrough 'A'	34	16	6	12	83	54	38
8. Wingate Albion	34	14	7	13	48	39	35
9. Wallsend Park Villa	34	15	3	16	49	59	33
10.Hebburn Argyle	34	13	6	15	38	62	32
11.Seaham Harbour	34	13	5	16	44	63	31
12.Spennymoor United	32	12	5	15	52	54	29
13.Workington	34	12	3	19	47	72	27
14.Shildon Athletic	34	11	3	20	50	64	25
15.Carlisle United	34	8	8	18	45	52	24
16.Jarrow	34	11	2	21	34	70	24
17.West Stanley	33	10	3	20	39	84	23
18.Sunderland Rovers	34	8	2	24	33	94	18

1911/12 Season: North-Eastern League

Date		Opponent	Result	Scorers
Sep	1	Sunderland Res.	1-0	Scanlon
	9	NEWCASTLE UTD RES.	0-2	
	23	WALLSEND PARK VILLA	2-1	Fenwick, Portlock
Oct	7	West Stanley	1-1	McIntyre
	21	GATESHEAD	1-1	Scanlon
	28	Wingate	2-2	McCleary, Portlock
Nov	4	SEAHAM HARBOUR	3-1	Portlock, McCleary(2)
	11	Shildon	3-1	Wilson(pen),McCleary(2,1pen)
	18	HEBBURN ARGYLE	3-1	Portlock(2), Scanlon
	25	Gateshead	0-2	
Dec	2	NEWCASTLE CITY	4-1	Hunter(3), Randall
	9	Hartlepools United	1-0	Scanlon(pen)
	23	Newcastle United Res.	0-4	
	25	MIDDLESBROUGH RES.	1-3	Ashridge
	26	NORTH SHIELDS ATH.	2-1	Pearson, Ashridge
	30	WINGATE	2-0	Scanlon, Hunter
Jan	1	SUNDERLAND ROYAL ROV.	6-0	* (see below)
	2	North Shields Athletic	0-1	
	6	Darlington	1-4	Hunter
	27	Hebburn Argyle	1-2	Portlock
Feb	10	HARTLEPOOLS UNITED	1-0	Rivers
	17	Seaham Harbour	2-1	Ashridge, Scanlon
	24	SUNDERLAND RES.	1-2	Pearson(pen)
Mar	2	Sunderland Royal Rovers	7-1	Hunter(3),Hogg,Smyth(p),Ashridge
	9	Jarrow Croft	3-1	Portlock(2), Ashridge
	16	WEST STANLEY	4-1	Hunter(3), Ashridge
	23	Wallsend Park Villa	2-1	Hunter, Portlock
	30	SPENNYMOOR UNITED	4-0	Ashridge(p),Hogg,Portlock,Jackson
Apr	5	JARROW CROFT	6-0	Portlock(2),Hogg(2),Hunter(2)
	6	Carlisle United	1-0	Hogg
	8	Middlesbrough Res.	0-2	
	9	DARLINGTON	0-1	
	13	SHILDON	4-0	Hunter(2), Portlock, Ashridge
	17	Newcastle City	1-1	Wllson(pen)
	20	CARLISLE UNITED	3-0	Ashridge(2), Hood

* Ashridge(2), Hunter, Lawrence (OG), Rivers, Jackson

A crowd of 11,000 attended the local derby at North Shields on 2 January.

Even with short travelling distances involved for North Eastern League matches the railways could not always be relied upon. A large crowd on 9 April had to wait a long time for visitors Darlington, who had been delayed and eventually arrived in taxis from Sunderland. (The following season South Shields were very late arriving at Middlesbrough).

1911/12 North-Eastern League

		P	W	D	L	F	A	Pts
1.	Middlesbrough 'A'	36	28	5	3	122	33	61
2.	Newcastle United 'A'	36	28	2	6	113	33	58
3.	Darlington	36	23	8	5	84	34	54
4.	Sunderland 'A'	36	21	5	10	99	52	47
5.	**SOUTH SHIELDS**	**36**	**21**	**4**	**11**	**73**	**43**	**46**
6.	Spennymoor United	36	18	6	12	62	57	42
7.	Newcastle City	36	16	9	11	62	43	41
8.	Gateshead Town	36	16	6	14	64	66	38
9.	Hartlepools United	36	14	8	14	62	50	36
10.	West Stanley	36	13	10	13	61	58	36
11.	North Shields Athletic	36	13	9	14	59	72	35
12.	Seaham Harbour	36	15	2	19	52	67	32
13.	Hebburn Argyle	36	11	9	16	56	54	31
14.	Wingate Albion	36	9	11	16	41	84	29
15.	Jarrow	36	10	7	19	52	87	27
16.	Shildon Athletic	36	9	6	21	62	97	24
17.	Carlisle United	36	7	6	23	27	98	20
18.	Wallsend Park Villa	36	8	3	25	43	93	19
19.	Sunderland Rovers	36	2	4	30	42	125	10

1912/13 Season: North-Eastern League

Date		Opponent	Score	Scorers
Sep	7	Carlisle United	6-1	Thornle(4), Hood,Bowerbank(OG)
	11	JARROW CROFT	3-0	Portlock, Hood(2)
	14	Wallsend Park Villa	4-0	Thornley(3), Portlock
	21	GATESHEAD	3-0	Bridgett, Hall(pen), Portlock
Oct	5	Sunderland Res.	0-1	
	19	SHILDON	2-1	Hogg, Thornley
	26	SEAHAM HARBOUR	5-0	Thornley(3),Phillipson,Brooks
Nov	9	Hartlepools United	4-0	Thornley,Hogg,McConnell,Phillipson
	23	Wingate Albion	3-0	Bridgett, Portlock, McConnell
Dec	7	Gateshead	5-1	Clark(OG),Thornley(3), Portlock
	25	CARLISLE UNITED	6-1	Thornley(3),Hood(2),Portlock
	26	North Shields Athletic	1-2	Thornley
	30	Newcastle United Res.	2-2	Portlock, Brookes(pen)
Jan	1	Houghton Rovers	2-2	Phillipson, Thornley
	2	NORTH SHIELDS ATHLETIC	4-0	Portlock,Wilson,Bridgett(p),Hogg
	4	WALLSEND PARK VILLA	5-1	Thornley(4), Young
Feb	1	Shildon	3-2	Hood, Thornley(2)
	5	Darlington	0-3	
	15	WEST STANLEY	4-2	Portlock,Brookes(2),Hindmarch
	22	MIDDLESBROUGH RES.	1-1	Hogg
Mar	1	Seaham Harbour	4-1	Hogg, Portlock, Brooks
	5	Newcastle City	0-0	
	8	HARTLEPOOLS UNITED	4-0	Thornley,Portlock(2),A.Bridgett
	12	WINGATE ALBION	5-0	E.Bridgett(pen),Portlock(3),Orr
	15	NEWCASTLE UTD RES.	2-0	Hogg, Thornley
	21	HOUGHTON ROVERS	1-1	Brookes(pen)
	22	Spennymoor United	3-1	Portlock(2), Hamilton
	24	SUNDERLAND ROVERS	3-0	Portlock, Hamilton(2,1pen)
	25	HEBBURN ARGYLE	3-0	A.Bridgett(3)
	29	DARLINGTON	0-0	
Apr	5	SUNDERLAND RES.	1-0	Thornley
	9	SPENNYMOOR UNITED	1-0	Hamilton
	12	Hebburn Argyle	2-2	Brookes, E.Hall
	16	Middlesbrough Res.	1-0	Hamilton
	19	West Stanley	3-1	Thornley(2), Brookes(pen)
	23	NEWCASTLE CITY	2-0	Raine, Portlock
	26	Sunderland Rovers	3-1	Thornley(2), Hamilton(pen)

1912 marks the beginning of a unique period in the history of South Shields Football Club. For the next three seasons they seem to have had access to unlimited supplies of money and spent much of it on buying established Football League players in a determined attempt to gain League membership. A notable acquisition was player manager Arthur Bridgett from Sunderland. From Stoke came goalkeeper Arthur Cartlidge and half-back Jock Grieve but it was from Manchester City that the club signed the remarkable Irvine Thornley. This Derbyshire born centre-forward had been scoring consistently for City for seven years and when confronted by weaker defences he was merciless.

These players were paid First Division wages and the club spent much money on ground improvements. However the 1912-13 season was something of a disappoint-ment. Darlington finished ahead of South Shields and an application to join the Football League in 1913 was a complete failure. Not one solitary vote was forth-coming.

1912/13 North-Eastern League							
	P	W	D	L	F	A	Pts
1. Darlington	38	31	4	3	116	23	66
2. SOUTH SHIELDS	38	27	7	4	103	30	61
3. Middlesbrough Reserves	38	26	6	6	102	40	58
4. Sunderland Reserves	38	26	5	7	100	48	57
5. Newcastle United Reserves	38	24	5	9	109	47	53
6. Spennymoor United	38	19	6	13	80	61	44
7. Shildon	38	17	9	12	79	69	43
8. Houghton Rovers	38	15	9	14	53	64	39
9. Wallsend	38	14	10	14	83	71	38
10. North Shields Athletic	38	15	7	16	72	78	37
11. Newcastle City	38	15	7	16	48	62	37
12. Hartlepools United	38	15	6	17	69	66	36
13. Hebburn Argyle	38	12	6	20	49	75	30
14. Carlisle United	38	12	5	21	61	98	29
15. Seaham Harbour	38	10	7	21	48	77	27
16. Jarrow	38	10	5	23	52	86	25
17. West Stanley	38	7	10	21	54	94	24
18. Sunderland rovers	38	7	8	23	39	79	22
19. Gateshead Town	38	8	6	24	49	112	22
20. Wingate Albion	38	5	2	31	28	114	12

1913/14 Season: North-Eastern League

Date		Opponent	Score	Scorers
Sep	3	WEST STANLEY	7-0	Thornley(5), A.Bridgett(2)
	6	Hartlepools United	1-1	Anderson
	13	HEBBURN ARGYLE	1-0	Thornley
	17	West Stanley	1-0	Brookes
	20	Darlington	1-1	Thornley
	25	Carlisle United	2-0	A.Bridgett, Anderson
	27	CARLISLE UNITED	4-0	Anderson(2),McCullough,A.Bridgett
Oct	4	SUNDERLAND RES.	0-2	
	11	MIDDLESBROUGH RES.	4-2	Thornley(3), Keenlyside
	18	Hebburn Argyle	1-1	Johnson
	25	Sunderland Rovers	3-0	Thornley(2), A.Bridgett
Nov	1	Middlesbrough Res.	3-2	A.Bridgett(2), Keenlyside
	8	SPENNYMOOR UNITED	5-0	A.Bridgett(3),Brookes,Keenlyside
	15	Sunderland Res.	2-1	A.Bridgett(2)
	22	SUNDERLAND ROVERS	4-2	Thornley,Arthur,Keenlyside,A.Bridgett
Dec	20	Wallsend Park Villa	1-0	Arthur
	25	Houghton Rovers	3-0	Thornley(3)
	26	NORTH SHIELDS	2-2	Thornley, Keenlyside
	27	JARROW	2-0	Keenlyside, E.Hall
Jan	1	HOUGHTON ROVERS	7-0	Portlock,Thornley(4),Bridgett,McCullough
	2	North Shields	6-1	Anderson,Snaith,Thornley(3),Portlock
	3	HARTLEPOOLS UNITED	3-2	Keenlyside, Thornley, Bridgett
	17	WALLSEND PARK VILLA	5-1	A.Bridgett(2),Brookes(2),Keenlyside
Feb	14	Gateshead	11-4	Thornley(5),A.Bridgett(2), *
	21	NEWCASTLE UTD RES.	1-1	Anderson
	28	Newcastle City	2-0	Keenlyside, Portlock
Mar	11	SHILDON	4-1	Thornley(3), E.Hall
	14	Spennymoor United	4-1	Bridgett(2),Thornley,Anderson
	18	BLYTH SPARTANS	5-1	E.Hall,Anderson(2),Thornley(2)
	21	DARLINGTON	7-1	Thornley(3),Brookes(pen) +
Apr	1	Shildon	4-0	Hubbard(2),Thornley,Anderson
	10	JARROW	3-0	Hubbard,Brookes(p),Thornley
	11	NEWCASTLE CITY	3-0	Hubbard(2), Thornley
	13	SEAHAM HARBOUR	6-0	Hubbard(2),Thornley(2) #
	14	Seaham Harbour	2-0	Thornley(2)
	18	Blyth Spartans	3-1	Thornley(3)
	22	Newcastle Utd Res.	2-1	A.Bridgett, Anderson
	25	GATESHEAD	8-1	Hubbard(4), J.Hall <

Several more Football League players joined the club in 1913 and this time the results speak for themselves. To all intents and purposes South Shields were a Football League club playing in a minor League. Irvine Thornley's 55 goals comprised less than half of the club's total as the championship was won by a margin of 15 points.

Despite this spectacular showing South Shields' application to join the Football League was rejected out of hand at the 1914 Annual General Meeting. Only one vote was obtained.

Graver matters lay ahead. The last home match against Gateshead was preceded by a Durham Light Infantry military display and recruiting exercise (You might as well join up now lads. They'll be coming for you soon enough)

Additional goalscorers:
* Brookes(pen),Portlock(2),Anderson
+ Hubbard, Anderson, Bridgett
# Anderson, Arthur
< Portlock(2), A.Bridgett

1913/14 North-Eastern League

		P	W	D	L	F	A	Pts
1.	SOUTH SHIELDS	38	32	5	1	133	29	69
2.	Middlesbrough Reserves	38	23	8	7	99	37	54
3.	Newcastle United Reserves	38	24	5	9	91	40	53
4.	Darlington	38	20	10	8	72	43	50
5.	Sunderland Reserves	38	20	8	10	83	55	48
6.	Blyth Spartans	38	19	7	12	71	51	45
7.	Hartlepools United	38	17	10	11	68	37	44
8.	Shildon	38	18	3	17	54	60	39
9.	Gateshead Town	38	17	5	16	58	76	39
10.	Hebburn Argyle	38	14	11	13	55	50	39
11.	Jarrow	38	12	10	16	55	63	34
12.	North Shields Athletic	38	11	10	17	57	81	32
13.	Carlisle United	38	11	10	17	48	84	32
14.	Spennymoor United	38	10	11	17	60	63	31
15.	Newcastle City	38	7	16	15	34	57	30
16.	Sunderland Rovers	38	10	10	18	46	67	30
17.	West Stanley	38	13	3	22	54	87	29
18.	Houghton Rovers	38	11	2	25	38	81	24
19.	Seaham Harbour	38	7	8	23	30	73	22
20.	Wallsend	38	5	6	27	44	115	16

1914/15 Season: North-Eastern League

Date	Opponent	Score	Scorers
Sep 5	ASHINGTON	3-0	Thornley(3)
9	West Stanley	1-2	Thornley
12	Newcstle Utd Res.	4-1	Thornley(2), Hubbard(2)
19	NEWCASTLE UTD RES.	3-1	Hubbard,A.Bridgett,Keenlyside
26	Wallsend	3-0	Keenlyside, A.Bridgett,Thornley
Oct 3	GATESHEAD	4-0	Lewis, Thornley(3)
24	Darlington	3-2	Hubbard(2), A.Bridgett
31	SUNDERLAND RES.	3-0	Hubbard(2), Thornley
Nov 7	DARLINGTON	2-1	Thornley(pen), Bridgett
14	SHILDON	1-1	Keenlyside
21	Sunderland Res.	2-1	Thornley, Whittingham
28	Middlesbrough Res.	2-3	Thornley, Whitttingham
Dec 5	MIDDLESBROUGH RES.	3-0	Whttingham(2), Robinson
25	HARTLEPOOLS UNITED	6-2	Keenlyside(2pens),Thornley*
26	North Shields	7-1	Portlock,A.Bridgett+
28	Jarrow	7-2	Lewis,(Thornley(4),Keenlyside(2pens)
Jan 1	HOUGHTON ROVERS	12-0	Burrell(3),Reside,A.Bridgett(2)#
2	NORTH SHIELDS	9-2	Thornley(4),Lewis(2) ~
4	WEST STANLEY	5-2	Thornley(4), A.Bridgett
16	BLYTH SPARTANS	4-0	Thornley(2),Reside,A.Bridgett
23	Gateshead	6-1	Robinson,Whittingham <
Feb 6	Shildon	1-1	B.Hall
13	HEBBURN ARGYLE	8-0	Thornley(2) Little (OG) ~
20	SUNDERLAND ROVERS	7-0	Thornley(6,1p),Whittingham
27	Blyth Spartans	1-0	Burrell
Mar 6	Hebburn Argyle	1-1	A.Bridgett
13	Hartlepools United	3-0	J.Hall, Reside, Whittingham
17	Newcastle City	2-1	Thornley, Whittingham
20	JARROW	12-0	Whittingham(6),Thornley(5),Bridgett
27	SPENNYMOOR UNITED	5-0	Thornley,Cowie,Whittingham(3)
Apr 2	WALLSEND	8-1	Thornley(3),Whittingham(3),Low,B.Hall
3	NEWCASTLE CITY	5-2	Thornley(2),Whittingham(2),A.Bridgett

War or no War the football season went ahead as planned with some understandable public criticism being levelled at the players.

Even more goals this time with Irvine Thornley's 65 being supplemented by an ex-Chelsea player 'Dickie' Whittingham who managed 35.

The Wednesday afternoon match at Newcastle City's Brough Park ground was watched by an attendance of 13.

At the end of the season Irvine Thornley retired to manage a local theatre and football closed down for the duration of the War.

Additional goalscorers:
*   Whittingahm(2),A.Bridgett
+   Thornley(3) ,Whittingham(2)
#   Thornley(4,1pen), J.Hall
~   Keenlyside(p) ,Whittingham,A.Bridgett
^   Whittingham(3), Ling (OG), Bridgett
<   Thornley,A.Bridgett, Dawson (OG)
~   Whittingham(4),A.Bridgett

1914/15 North-Eastern League

		P	W	D	L	F	A	Pts
1	SOUTH SHIELDS	38	32	4	3	160	34	68
2	Middlesbrough Reserves	38	28	5	5	131	35	61
3	Newcastle United Reserves	39	26	6	6	138	43	58
4	Darlington	38	25	4	9	109	38	54
5	West Stanley	38	24	4	10	79	44	52
6	Sunderland Reserves	38	18	9	11	86	50	45
7	Hartlepools United	38	16	11	11	74	57	43
8	North Shields Athletic	38	19	5	14	67	63	43
9	Ashington	38	15	11	12	60	65	41
10	Sunderland Rovers	38	17	4	17	74	79	38
11	Spennymoor United	38	12	9	17	40	82	33
12	Shildon	38	11	9	18	70	58	31
13	Hebburn Argyle	38	12	6	20	50	73	30
14	Jarrow	38	10	10	18	46	85	30
15	Blyth Spartans	38	10	9	19	49	75	29
16	Houghton Rovers	38	11	4	23	43	123	28
17	Carlisle United	38	8	7	23	50	108	23
18	Newcastle City	38	8	5	25	43	87	21
19	Gateshead Town	38	8	3	27	52	121	19
20	Wallsend	38	6	3	29	44	136	15

(1919/20) Post War Optimism Justified

The management of the South Shields Football Club were dissatisfied with their status as a North Eastern League Club. The championship of this competition had been won very convincingly in each of the two seasons before normal organised football was suspended and the logical step forward would seem the Second Division of the Football League. Several clubs in the league were based in towns with smaller populations than that of South Shields. As the world returned to a semblance of normality the club's finances were augmented by three friendly matches against Middlesbrough, Leeds City and Bradford City over the Christmas and New Year period of 1918-19. Although these matches resulted in defeats of 4-2, 3-1, and 6-1 respectively the aggregate attendance of 30,000 paying £800 was very encouraging. The club then participated in a hastily arranged "Victory League" comprising North Eastern clubs while the manager, Mr Jack Tinn, toured the country visiting every Football League club canvassing support.

A prospectus was issued pointing out that the area was enjoying great and increasing prosperity (a rather dubious claim) and extolling the virtues of the Horsley Hill enclosure; £2,000 had been spent on improving the pitch and providing dressing room and stand accommodation. Reference was made to the successful North Eastern League seasons - the average match takings during the 1913-14 season had been £173 - and pre-war meetings with League clubs in the FA Cup had also produced satisfactory "gates". These efforts bore fruit when the Football League met at Manchester on 10 March. The number of League clubs was increased from 40 to 44 and of the seven applicants for membership Coventry City polled 35 votes, West Ham United 32 votes, and Rotherham County and South Shields both 28. Unsuccessful applicants were Port Vale with 27 votes and Rochdale and Southport each with 7. As luck would have it Port Vale would join South Shields in the Second Division the following season anyway.

News of the elevation of South Shields in the football world was welcomed warmly in the district. *"A well deserved honour"* said the Shields Daily Gazette. Much work remained to be done before the first League match in August and during the summer major alterations were made to the ground, increasing capacity and extending covered accommodation.

In respect of the latter it seems that a far greater proportion of the Horsley Hill crowd was

George Keenlyside

sheltered from the rain than was the case with their opposite numbers at Roker and St James's Parks several decades later. With the club comfortably in credit at the bank the urgent task of strengthening the playing squad was well under way.

The only pre-war players available were George Keenlyside, who was to remain a fine servant of the club for several years, and Henry Dreyer. The bulk of the new side was made up of local men including the greatest of all South Shields players, Warney Cresswell, who was signed in the face of competition from Tottenham Hotspur (for whom he had guested during the war) and Newcastle United. Forays across the border brought back Archie Jack from Falkirk and the not very Scottish sounding Henry Higginbotham from St. Mirren.

Pre-season friendlies and practice matches were played and on Friday 29 August the South Shields players travelled to London to play their first League game at Fulham.

Accompanying them on the train was the Newcastle United team en route for Highbury and the journey was described as a *"merry"* one. Fulham were not an entirely unknown quantity having played at Horsley Hill in an FA Cup-tie in 1915 and four survivors from that game were among those facing South Shields at Craven Cottage. The result, as before, was a Fulham victory this time by the only goal of the game. South Shields gave a good account of themselves being strong in defence but failing to make use of scoring chances.

The first home fixture was much anticipated and on Monday evening, 1 September, Birmingham came to Horsley Hill. The weather was not kind, with heavy rain and wind, but this did not deter 15,000 people from attending. The match proved to be something of a disappointment. The first half saw many South Shields attacking moves come to nothing but after the interval Birmingham dominated play and it was only the brilliance of South Shields goalkeeper Ernie Hoffman which denied them what seemed to be a certain victory. However, with time running out and quite against the run of play Henry Higginbotham passed to Archie Roe who after a brief scramble in the goalmouth scored with the last kick of the match. The crowd went wild with joy and even goalkeeper Hoffman left his post to join in the celebrations and give the goalscorer *"an affectionate embrace"*.

So South Shields had won their spurs, albeit luckily. Some reports were almost scathing but all agreed that what the game lacked in skill it made up for in excitement. It is significant that Archie Roe's winning goal so impressed Birmingham that they signed him shortly afterwards. So as well as being the first South Shields player to score a League goal he was also the first to be transferred after a good performance. The first of many.

The return game with Fulham took place on the following Saturday. A larger crowd, this time of 17,000, was treated to an altogether better game and another home victory. *"What a roar went up*

when Bell got possession and flashed the leather into the net for the first Shields goal" reported the Sunday Sun continuing *"Frith created another furore by scoring a lovely goal with a drive at fully 30 yards range"*. A pleasant afternoon was had by all and there seems to have been some support for Fulham who were to remain popular visitors to Horsley Hill. The match was mostly controlled by a Newcastle linesman as the Manchester referee had missed a connection at York and did not arrive until half-time.

On the following Monday the popular South Shields captain George Keenlyside married in his nearby home town of Jarrow with Ernie Hoffman acting as a groomsman. After receiving a gift of cutlery from the club the happy couple left for London. The honeymoon must have been a short one as the bridegroom was back in the team at Birmingham on Wednesday evening. Perhaps it wasn't the only honeymoon that was over as South Shields suffered their first significant defeat by four goals to nil.

Another visit to London followed this time to White Hart Lane where South Shields were a shade unlucky to lose 2-0 to a Tottenham Hotspur side whose victory was their fifth out of five. Their sixth out of six was accomplished without difficulty at Horsley Hill a week later in another match in which the referee arrived to find they'd started without him.

Around this time another visitor to the North East was being regarded with an amused eye by the local press. One "Pussyfoot" Johnson, an American gentleman, was addressing sparse gatherings in Newcastle and Sunderland in his attempt to extend Prohibition to Britain after its recent adoption in his native land. Good-natured scorn was being heaped upon him in almost every newspaper as he pursued his lonely campaign to make the world a better place. The world became a better place anyway. A man protested at a Tyneside Magistrates Court that *"the Government did not pay me anything when my three sons were killed in the war, yet you fine me five pounds for shooting a bird"*.

At the same time the cartmen employed by a rural council near Newcastle threatened to withdraw their labour. Cartmen? The contents of their carts becomes apparent when their employers reminded them that if they went on strike they would gravely endanger the health of the district. Dreadful days. Rejoice that they are gone.

Industrial unrest was prevalent and on Saturday 27 September a national railway strike began. South Shields were once again in London and had troubles enough. A 4-0 defeat by Clapton Orient, an injury to George Keenlyside which was to keep him out of the game for a year, and now there was the problem of getting home. A friendly sea captain came to the rescue. Set to sail for the Tyne he offered the club the run of his steamer.

The whole of Sunday was spent on the choppy North Sea (no longer the German Ocean) and the voyage which *"did not pass without incident"* ended with the reluctant sailors disembarking from the good ship Dalton at 4.30am on Monday. Reports of their dis-comfort must have caused a wry smile in a town which was the home of many seamen.

The strike continued until the following Monday and in an age when long distance travel was almost exclusively done by rail the football world was very seriously affected. There were grumbles about coach firms profiteering as they carried football teams and some sympathy was expressed for Clapton Orient as they arrived at Horsley Hill after a tiring journey for a match, which South Shields won 2-0. Still the referee (of necessity a local man from Tynemouth) arrived on time, which was more than could be said for his two predecessors on days when the trains were running.

One of the scorers in the victory over Clapton Orient was George Lillycrop, a local man who had been a member of Barnsley's Cup winning team of 1912 and who had been signed from Bolton Wanderers. Now nearing the end of his playing career he was to give South Shields good service as a trainer for some years.

Another dramatic event was looming. The Leeds City club had fallen foul of the Football Association because of irregularities and in an age of severe punishments the club was disbanded. The effect on South Shields was twofold - an immediate inconvenience and a long term benefit. Firstly there was the fact that they had been due to play Leeds City at Elland Road on the following Saturday and would now be without a fixture. In the end South Shields arranged a friendly with Hartlepools United which was won 3-0.

Secondly the assets of the now defunct Leeds City club included all their players. A unique event took place at the Metropole Hotel, Leeds, on Friday 17 October when thirty League clubs attended an auction for these players.

Willis Walker

South Shields were rep-resented and bid successfully for two men, William "Pop" Hopkins and goalkeeper Willis Walker. The latter purchase was the best the club ever made.

Port Vale were admitted into the League to take the place of Leeds City and their first match was at Horsley Hill. It seems rather patronising of the local press to refer to Port Vale as newcomers lacking the experience of a senior League club like South Shields - all six weeks of it - but be that as it may South Shields won 2-0 before an encouragingly high crowd of 17,000.

A rather lean spell followed with only one point from two games with Bury, a goalless draw at Nottingham Forest and then Port Vale gained their revenge winning 1-0 at Hanley.

On 15 November a heavy fall of snow blanketed Tyneside causing the postponement of the Newcastle United v Middlesbrough match.

Seeing the chance of an increased gate in the absence of a counter attraction the South Shields directors employed the latest technology and sent *"a small army of sandwichmen"* round the district announcing that the match with Nottingham Forest was definitely on. It seems to have worked as 14,000 people were treated to a high scoring game. South Shields won 5-2 in conditions which did little for *"the spotless white jerseys and shorts"* of the home team.

The acid test for support came two weeks later when Leicester City's visit coincided with the Newcastle versus Sunderland match and the crowd of 12,000 who witnessed a 2-0 victory must have been regarded as quite satisfactory. The South Shields board acted ambitiously in trying to sign Stan Seymour who was then playing for Morton. Instead he opted for a distinguished career with Newcastle United and he will reappear in these pages.

Away form had been very poor and South Shields had only scored once in eight away games. The first away victory came at Barnsley on 6 December. Christmas and New Year passed with a defeat and a victory against Stockport County and two goalless draws with Wolverhampton Wanderers. The home match with Wolves was particularly disappointing as between these two drab encounters Wolves had been defeated 10-3 at Hull. Two days later Hull City themselves visited Horsley Hill. The match attracted a record crowd, partly because of Hull's recent double figure score but mostly because they were due to play Sunderland in the FA Cup at Roker Park the following week. A large contingent made the short trip from Wearside.

The record crowd saw the game of a lifetime. After ten minutes half back Henry Dreyer put South Shields ahead but there was little to choose between the two sides and Hull City played like League leaders. The second half was a different story.

Charlton added a second for South Shields after 54 minutes and Hull City pulled one back through Lee three minutes later.

Young Jack Oxberry sent in a powerful shot which Hull defender Edleston tried to stop but merely succeeded in deflecting into his own goal.

Jack Oxberry

Billy Charlton scored his second goal of the match on 75 minutes and completed his hat trick shortly afterwards, but South Shields had not finished yet as J W Smith scored twice to make the final score 7-1.

Jack Smith

The Sunday Sun waxed lyrical. *"It was difficult to believe as the Tynesiders piled on goal after goal that it was the same side with two exceptions which had played so poorly against the Wolves on New Years Day.... From stem to stern South Shields were splendid. There was not a weakness anywhere.... South Shields left no room for criticism, they were tip top. J W Smith was the best forward but the whole five were individually and collectively clever. A. Smith and Oxberry steadily improve and will do even better later. Charlton as a centre forward was a revelation. The half back line was faultless, and the full backs though not brilliant made no mistakes.... Walker in goal was excellent."*

Who could now doubt that South Shields were worthy of a place in the Football League?

After this match they were a power in it, a side to be feared. Some of the names in this glowing report demand further introduction. Jack Smith, the best forward, was to be the leading scorer and had a distinguished career ahead of him. Jack Oxberry a local man signed from Boldon Villa was to be a South Shields stalwart for many years. Billy Charlton the revelatory centre forward here scoring his only South Shields hat trick but always a useful player for numerous League clubs, and goalkeeper Willis Walker who often won applause at away grounds as well as at Horsley Hill for his fine performances.

The following week Liverpool were due at Horsley Hill in the first round of the FA Cup. The visit of this famous club in the wake of the peak performance just described should have ensured another high attendance but ill fortune intervened in the form of atrocious weather and the gate was a mere 7,790 - considerably lower than for any League match so far - the game having been in doubt until shortly before kick off time. The state of the pitch was deplorable to begin with and worsened steadily with the players wading ankle deep in slush. After 53 minutes Woods managed to pierce a Liverpool defence *"merciless in its methods"* but Liverpool's Lewis equalised with an easy chance and there was no further score. On the Tuesday South Shields journeyed to Anfield for the replay and despite splendid defensive work lost 2-0.

So the first venture into the FA Cup as a League club brought South Shields no joy other than a share of the replay gate of 39,000. Two features will recur in this story. Firstly the legendary "Lady Luck" seemed disinclined to smile on the club. Secondly the South Shields pitch seems to have been an awful one. Again and again match reports describe it and photographs confirm it as being a mudbath and not just in abnormal weather.

As if to illustrate the changing fortunes of football South Shields lost the return match at Hull 3-0. (An attempt to cash in on the happy memories of the 7-1 match failed when South Shields arranged a home friendly against Hull

on a vacant cup-tie date of Saturday, 6 March. On this occasion City won 1-0 before a small crowd).

Before that result, however, much of value was accomplished in the League. Three points were taken from struggling Coventry City and on 7 February the club won fresh laurels when they visited Huddersfield Town, who were chasing Tottenham Hotspur at the top of the division and who had dismissed Newcastle from the FA Cup a week previously at St. James's Park.

In a fine performance South Shields twice took the lead through goals from Lillycrop and Woods but had to be content with a single point. A large crowd assembled at Horsley Hill the following week but this time Huddersfield proved to be too strong winning 2-1. Then it was Blackpool. A convincing 3-0 victory at Bloomfield Road so pleased the South Shields directors that they treated the players to a supper and a musical evening.

Bill Charlton

This seems to have had the desired affect as the score was improved upon at Horsley Hill when "old man" George Lillycrop scored four goals with Jack Smith and Bill Charlton adding one each against a Blackpool side again unable to reply.

It would be fair to add at this point that the directors of South Shields Football Club never seem to have stinted in their treatment of the players. Many treats and excursions were reported in the local press. Generally the club seems to have been a rather good natured organisation.

Four points from two games with Blackpool was followed by no points from two games with Bristol City who had reached the semi-final of the FA Cup. In a midweek game at Horsley Hill the visitors won 2-0 but were described as being *"almost crude and certainly not sportsmanlike"*. After City had completed the double over them at Ashton Gate at the weekend South Shields ventured into South Wales losing 3-1 in a friendly match against Mid-Rhondda at Tonypandy and travelling home on the Tuesday. Much interest was shown in the visit of West Ham United who were beaten 3-0 before a near record crowd basking in ideal weather.

Matches over Easter proved interesting, especially a game against Rotherham County on the Saturday. Rotherham fielded Billy Frith who had played for South Shields earlier in the season but who expected and gave no quarter in a rough match which South Shields won 6-2. Remarkably Rotherham had been winning 2-1 after 75 minutes. This match was sandwiched between two games with Lincoln City both of which were drawn. The following Saturday "Wanderer" of the Shields Football Gazette reminded his readers that Lincoln City, who were in danger of having to apply for re-election, were old friends of South Shields, and that their single vote had been enough to tip the balance when South Shields were elected into the League by a one vote majority over Port Vale, therefore nobody should begrudge them a well deserved point at Horsley Hill.

What are we to infer from this? Is it a hint from a source close to the club that the "Old Pals Act" (which was old then) was in force? If so it was not enough to save Lincoln who failed to be re-elected and had to leave the League temporarily. In any case rival strugglers Coventry City could hardly complain.

The story has been well told elsewhere of that club's victory over Bury on the last day of the season, which resulted in a League enquiry after three years of rumours. Long afterwards a participant recalled an apologetic Bury player appearing in the Coventry dressing room at half time to say that the deal might fall through because Coventry were playing so badly it was almost impossible not to beat them.

We haven't heard the last of stories like this. If South Shields did return a favour on that long ago Good Friday then was this wicked world any the wickeder? On Easter Monday at Sincil Bank the locals cheered sportingly when Willis Walker saved a penalty thus depriving Lincoln City of a rare victory.

(1920/21) The Usual Twenty Thousand

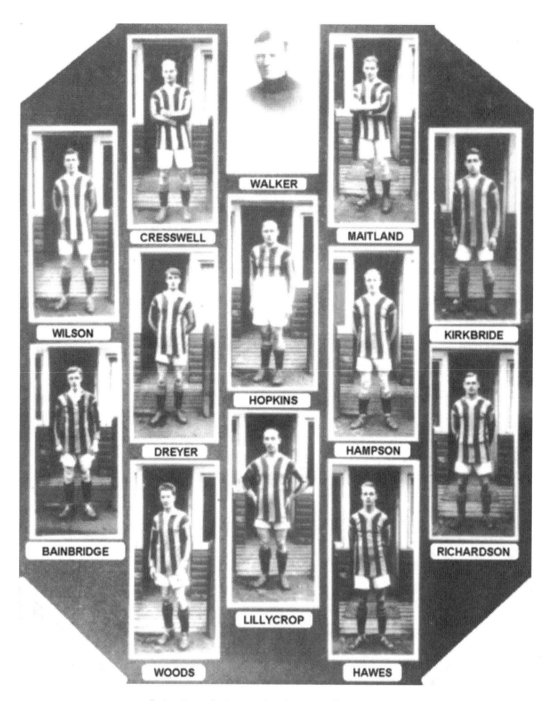

~ Selection of players for the 1920/21 season ~

The experiment had been a success. The South Shields Football Club had more than held their own in the Second Division finishing ninth out of twenty-two. Three high scores - a seven and two sixes - had been on the right side of the score sheet though the away record was unimpressive. Gates were satisfactorily high averaging 14,975, a figure surpassed only by four other Second Division clubs - promoted Tottenham Hotspur, Birmingham, West Ham United and (surprisingly) Coventry City. £21,095 had been taken in gate money leaving a profit after expenses of more than £1,700. A *"colossal"* offer of £10,000 for three players had been resisted.

Arthur 'Tricky' Hawes

Further ground improvements had been made with extensions to the stand and more covered accommodation provided. Some players had left, others had been signed including Arthur "Tricky" Hawes from Norwich City and Simpson Bainbridge from Preston North End.

There would be four new opponents in 1920-21 with two famous old clubs, Notts County and Sheffield Wednesday, having been relegated from the First Division whilst Cardiff City and the newly formed Leeds United club had replaced Lincoln City and Grimsby Town.

Once again Birmingham were the first visitors to Horsley Hill and a crowd of twenty thousand went home happy after a convincing 3-0 home victory, two of the goals scored by new boy Hawes. Leeds United had lost their first League game at Port Vale and on Tuesday evening South Shields were their first ever visitors. South Shields won 2-1, all the goals coming in the first fifteen minutes.

The North Mail put the result down to *"indecision on the part of Leeds defenders"*. South Shields came in for fulsome praise however: *"A sound and solid side. Walker was clean and confident in all his work, while the backs' work was without blemish, their kicking being extremely clean. Hopkins was the outstanding half back of the match and his feeding of the wings was exemplary"*. Elland Road regulars must have wished that these two had never gone under the hammer at the Metropole Hotel.

A week later (after a draw at Birmingham) it was time to entertain Leeds United at Horsley Hill. This match resulted in a 3-0 victory with another two goals from Hawes while Simpson Bainbridge - another Metropole auction lot - added a third. The game was not one-sided though. The North Mail noted that Leeds were *"out for blood.... Free kicks constituted the principle feature of the early stages, not all for fouls it should be stated at once, the majority being for dangerous play. Neither were the penalties all against one side, because one or two of the home men were not inclined to take things lying down.... Referee Wilkinson handled the game firmly and after making it quite plain to both sides that he was not in the humour to stand any nonsense he succeeded in inducing the men to play rather more football."*

DIVISION II.					Goals.		
	P.	W.	L.	D.	F.	A.	P.
South Shields	6	4	0	2	18	5	10
Stoke	6	3	1	2	12	5	8
Cardiff City	6	3	1	2	11	6	8
West Ham United	6	3	1	2	7	1	8
Notts County	6	3	1	2	8	6	8
Clapton Orient	7	3	2	2	12	10	8
Blackpool	7	3	2	3	12	8	7
Bury	6	3	2	1	11	9	7
Hull City	6	3	3	1	8	9	7
Fulham	6	2	2	1	9	6	6
Port Vale	6	1	1	4	5	6	6
Bristol City	6	2	2	2	7	8	6
Leeds United	6	2	3	1	3	10	5
Rotherham County	6	1	2	3	6	8	5
Sheffield Wednesday	5	1	1	3	2	3	5
Leicester City	6	2	3	1	8	11	5
Birmingham	6	1	3	2	8	9	4
Barnsley	6	0	2	4	5	7	4
Wolverhampton Wanderers	6	2	4	0	5	8	4
Nottingham Forest	6	1	4	2	5	8	4
Coventry City	6	1	3	2	3	9	4
Stockport County	6	1	4	1	10	17	3

South Shields top the Division.

Whether or not the crowd shared this reporter's ability to distinguish between fouls and dangerous play, they seem to have been well satisfied as another large crowd variously

Hampson's free-kick is saved by the goalkeeper in the Barnsley match

estimated as sixteen or twenty thousand assembled on Saturday to see another victory over Barnsley with Hawes bagging his now monotonous brace. South Shields now topped the Second Division table and, with a single Hawes goal victory over Rotherham County, were now the only undefeated club in the country. Heady days and no lack of ambition. Land used as allotments at one end of the ground was purchased by the club and work was immediately set in hand to increase the capacity of the ground.

The first defeat came at Rotherham by the odd goal in nine in heavy weather. Coventry City were then beaten 4-1 at Horsley Hill. Supporters who forked out a penny for the Football Gazette the following week - no mean consideration at a time when 9,000 miners were on strike locally - found only the briefest report of the opening stages of the return match at Highfield Road because of *"telephonic difficulties"*. The match itself was just as disappointing with Coventry winning 1-0, but the club returned with Coventry's *"brilliant"* centre forward Richard Parker for whom they paid £1,000.

Like many players who arrived at South Shields, Parker was a North Easterner returning home. A native of Stockton, he had played in the First Division for Sunderland the previous season before Coventry had secured his services for £1,500. Coventry must have thought their money was well spent as they had failed to score in eleven successive matches earlier in the season and Parker proceeded to score 9 goals in 16 games. Despite Parker's brilliance Coventry were still failing to score very many but it was probably the consolation goal he scored at Horsley Hill on 9 October that led to his transfer. South Shields recouped some of their money immediately as the crowd for the next home game exceeded 20,000 and for the first time the gates had to be closed.

The expensive new signing did not disappoint, in fact he scored a hat trick (one a penalty) with Tricky Hawes scoring two more and Woods putting a sixth past a troubled elderly Port Vale goalkeeper who could do little right. Another feature of this memorable game was the return of the old favourite George Keenlyside after a year on the sidelines. Port Vale were no mean opponents and the press thought that the scoreline flattered South Shields. A week later the double was accomplished with South Shields winning 2-0 at Port Vale.

The following week another large crowd assembled at Horsley Hill but this time the visitors, Nottingham Forest, won by the only goal of the game. Impressively South Shields won the return game at Nottingham a week later.

Could South Shields really make the First Division?. Three more points from Hull City (a goalless draw at home watched by *"the usual twenty thousand - the ground which has a capacity of 24,000 seemed pretty well full"* - and an away victory) kept hopes alive. No points from two games with Wolves, a goalless draw at Stockport and a narrow defeat at Bury on Christmas Day suggested that the dream was fading. Still crowds of twenty thousand or so gathered at Horsley Hill on Boxing Day and New Years Day to witness victories over Bury and Stockport.

The expensive signing Richard Parker disappeared from the scene just before Christmas though why he should have done so is a mystery. After his dramatic debut he played eight further League matches scoring twice. After the match at Stockport on 18 December (in which there is no suggestion that he sustained an injury) he only played for the first team once more - in a cup-tie.

Top position had long been relinquished and the magic of the FA Cup asserted itself. The Southern League had now evolved into the Third Division of the Football League and one of its most attractive sides, Portsmouth (the last champions of the "old" Southern League) visited Horsley Hill in the first round. There was not a weak spot in the South Shields team which disposed of a typical South coast collection of Northerners and Scotsmen by three goals to nil in *"a most attractive game productive of many thrills"*.

The only disappointment was the size of the crowd - officially 15,510. This would undoubtedly have been larger had not Newcastle and Sunderland been at home. In fact Newcastle had been drawn away but their opponents Nottingham Forest had agreed to switch the tie to St James's Park in the hope of a bigger gate. South Shields could justifiably feel aggrieved at Forest's action. Faced with similar temptation in later years they would show more consideration to their own supporters at times when they could ill afford to.

Another Third Division (South) club Luton Town were drawn to play at Horsley Hill in the second round and this match was anticipated with optimism. Despite having to compete with a Newcastle v Liverpool tie the attendance record at Horsley Hill was broken. The Football Gazette estimated the crowd at 25,000 but the official figure was 21,003 paying £1,776-6-1. What a disappointment! South Shields were run ragged by a *"brilliant"* Luton side who included ex-Shieldsman Henry Higginbotham and who emerged victorious by four goals to nil.

This abrupt and unlooked for dismissal from the Cup at a time when promotion hopes had dwindled rather took the wind out of the sails of the team from that nautical town. For one thing it meant that *"the usual twenty thousand"* of only a few weeks before was now likely to be ten thousand or so. The lucrative Cup-tie with Luton had necessitated the postponement of the home League match with Clapton Orient to Wednesday afternoon. The inevitable low attendance, variously estimated as five or ten thousand, witnessed a 3-0 victory.

Star defender Warney Cresswell was absent from the home match against Blackpool on 12 March as he was playing for the Football League against the Scottish League at Highbury (in effect an international practice match). Forty-eight hours later he received his first international cap when he played for England against Wales at Cardiff. The experience seems to have been rather mixed. The Times informs us that he played well in the Inter-League match but that in the International the England defence *"mainly through the unreliability of Cresswell had some very anxious moments"*, so the difference in class must have been a problem. The match finished goalless however.

A lean run of nine games produced two single goal victories, two draws and five narrow defeats before a 4-3 victory over Leicester City ensued at Horsley Hill. Then came a long and tedious journey by road to Cardiff because of further railway troubles.

Despite Warney Cresswell's familiarity with Ninian Park the promotion chasing Welshmen won 1-0 and repeated their success a week later. A goalless draw at Fulham was watched by a gratifyingly high crowd considering that the FA Cup Final was being played a few minutes walk away at Stamford Bridge. On the way home South Shields stopped off at Norwich where they drew a match with City thus entitling them to hold the Norwich and Norfolk Charity Cup for six months. Never a dull moment.

For the return match with Fulham the crowd was back up round the 16,000 mark, chiefly one suspects because of interest in a visiting player. Barney Travers, a Sunderland man, had been transferred from his home town club just a few weeks earlier and had already scored 9 goals in 13 games for Fulham, which was hardly surprising as his impressive record at Roker Park had included two hat tricks. Anybody who came especially to see him saw an entertaining game which South Shields won 3-0 but Barney's own behaviour was decidedly odd. Again and again promising Fulham attacks were thwarted because Travers failed to stay onside. He succeeded in putting the ball into the net but was once again offside. Then he *"broke through, and tricking Cresswell, was only a few yards out with the goal at his mercy when he sent high over the bar."*

What can a man of his experience have been thinking about? Surely the offside laws must have been familiar to him. Anybody would think that he didn't want his London employers to win a match so near his own home. We shall hear more of Barney Travers in the corresponding match in 1921-22.

All that remained of the League season were the matches with West Ham United resulting in a 2-1 defeat at Upton Park, then on 7 May *"the season at Horsley Hill finished very quietly not to say timidly"* with a goalless draw.

In many ways this was the best season South Shields were to experience having led the Division for several weeks and having had a player capped for England. Certainly the generally high attendances would never be repeated. Not only were League and Cup games well supported but the reserve team playing in the North Eastern League were drawing gates of 4 - 5,000 regularly and much more for matches against Newcastle and Sunderland reserves. A "Northern Victory Cup" match against Sunderland (who won 1-0) in April had been watched by 17,000 and this figure was exceeded a week later for the final, Sunderland beating Middlesbrough 3-0 at Horsley Hill. A match between a combined North Eastern XI and a Players Union team was equally well supported.

The disappointments of the season had been the heavy Cup defeat by Luton and the unexplained dropping of the expensive signing Richard Parker. He was released to go to Wallsend shortly afterwards but returned to League soccer as a prolific scorer with other clubs, including Millwall where his record number of goals in a season stands to this day. Perhaps he was a quarrelsome character as there are suggestions that he left other clubs rather abruptly.

****

When the balance sheet was published in June the comment was made that the club would not be able to compete in the transfer market - and this in the season of *"the usual twenty thousand"*.

Oddities included:-
Hotel and travelling expenses: £2,797-8-2½ (Where on earth could that odd half penny have been spent?)
Compensation to allotment holders: £47-0-0
..... And strangest of all:-
Loss on purchase and sale of horse: £15-7-0!

(1921/22) The Goal Famine Begins

The Newcastle United full back Bill McCracken had perfected the offside trap to such a degree that goalscoring was becoming very difficult. Although his tactic was unpopular with opponents it found many imitators and in the early twenties the number of goals scored in all League matches declined dramatically. The problem became so acute that in 1925 a change was made in the offside law. At South Shields, as everywhere, high scoring games seemed to have become a thing of the past as a glance down the results tables for these years will confirm.

Another development in the football world in 1921 was the introduction of the Northern Section of the Third Division. With hindsight we know that this rather haphazard collection of small town clubs from the North Eastern, Central, Midland and Birmingham District Leagues and the Lancashire Combination was never to rival its Southern counterpart which was in effect the old Southern League comprising clubs from larger places with much greater potential. Even as the Northern Section was taking shape, doubts were being expressed as to its feasibility. It seems unlikely that clubs of the stature of South Shields, Barnsley and Rotherham County would have enthused as they seem to have regarded themselves as permanent Second Division members who, if the worst came to the worst, could plead for re-election. Now there was the spectre of relegation to contend with and it had already claimed wooden-spoonists Stockport County.

The number of Football League clubs in the North East now numbered eight and the 1921-22 season got off to a bright start when five of them won and three drew. South Shields fell into the latter category sharing the points at Hull, the scorer being centre forward Walter Casson, a summer signing from Blyth Spartans. A few days earlier South Shields had beaten First Division Middlesbrough but they had been playing cricket on that occasion.

Crowds of 18,000 saw a 1-1 draw with Stoke and a 1-0 victory in the return match with Hull. A high scoring 2-1 defeat in foul weather at Stoke was followed by a run of ten games which all ended 0-0, 0-1 or 1-1 so perhaps that conversion to cricket wasn't such a bad idea!

The problem was encapsulated in the match at Horsley Hill on 1 October when, despite South Shields 1-0 victory, the crowd *"voiced their dissatisfaction in no half hearted manner"*, and no wonder. The report in the Sunday Sun is worth quoting at length.

"Cope, the West Ham United left back was the star artist at the [offside trap] *game at first. It became almost pathetic to see the ease and simplicity with which the Shields forwards succumbed to his wiles. Then Cresswell gave evidence to all and sundry that Cope was not the only offside merchant on the field and between them they reduced the respective opposition to impotence for huge slices of the game"*.

Yet a week later a goalless draw at Leeds had Wanderer of the Shields Daily Gazette in raptures. *"It was a rousing encounter crammed with incident and productive of sparkling football while thrill after thrill was provided by the Shieldsmen in the later stages when they attacked with such persistency and determination that the home team was completely outplayed and out manoeuvred.... I have never seen the Seasiders give a more convincing display this season and their skilful and polished work, both in attack and defence, delighted beyond measure the enthusiastic band of supporters who made the journey to Leeds, while it did not fail to impress the remainder of the 20,000 spectators who witnessed the game"*.

Great stuff no doubt but the fifteenth match of the season was the first in which South Shields scored twice with a victory over Bristol City, the double being completed at Ashton Gate a week later.

The only two games all season in which both sides scored more than once occurred on Christmas Eve at Molineux where South Shields lost 3-2 to Wolves after being 2-0 ahead at half time and, an oasis in that desert season, when Barnsley were defeated 5-2 at Horsley Hill on the last day of the year.

Gates were falling now. In November the directors reduced the admission price for the stands but this did not please the patrons of the popular end whose shilling was the irreducible minimum permitted by the Football League. It seems to have been an attempt to sugar the pill as the most popular players were to be transferred soon. The club denied a rumour that Warney Cresswell was bound for Everton for £6,000 but the previous season's leading scorers left soon afterwards. Arthur Hawes to Sunderland (where he was a success) and Henry Woods to Newcastle (where he wasn't). In the case of Hawes the fee was later stated to be £1,750.

There was no Cup run that year, merely a long journey to Southampton for a 3-1 defeat. The Horsley Hill pitch continued to attract comment. For the Rotherham County match on 28 January it was, *"probably... never worse. For about 20 yards out from the east goal there stretched a black puddle in which the players were ankle deep, and pools of mud studded various parts of the field."* Failing light meant that the half time break had to be dispensed with *"much to the disgust of several of the players who were evidently anxious to get rid of the mud"* (Sunday Sun).

On Friday 3 March the inevitable happened and Warney Cresswell was finally transferred to Sunderland for a new world record transfer fee of £5,500. How did his depleted team mates react? Magnificently! They travelled to Hillsborough and showed Sheffield Wednesday how to play football with a scintillating 3-0 victory, the highlight of the season.

Some of the money received was spent on the purchase of Ernie Simms of Luton Town who was the leading scorer in the Southern section of the Third Division.

Like the newly departed Cresswell he had been capped once for England (against Ireland earlier in the season) and he was a native of the district. The return game with Sheffield Wednesday which attracted a good attendance was goalless as was Simms' midweek debut against Notts County.

The home game against Fulham was a fine one with the visitors pushing for promotion, *".... On Saturday's form South Shields have no superiors in the Second Division. There has not been a better exhibition of football at Horsley Hill and the Seasiders brilliant victory will rank among the finest of their achievements"* was Wanderer's verdict on the 1-0 win. The Second Division's leading scorer was old Roker favourite Barney Travers who had managed to pierce tight defences seventeen times for Fulham that season. In this match he seemed quite subdued. South Shields full backs Ridley and Maitland *"fastened on to Travers.... Maitland stopped Travers when the Fulham leader looked like doing some damage"*. Perhaps words were passed in these duels. Perhaps Travers knew the game was up. Maitland had already reported to his directors that Travers had offered him a sum of money to fall down to allow Fulham to score. Barney Travers had scored his last goal and was playing his last match.

The matter was dealt with very swiftly. A week or so later Alf Maitland accompanied the South Shields directors to London and gave his evidence. A joint Football League and Football Association commission then met at Birmingham and suspended the culprit for all time. In later years Travers was to maintain that his only sin was to break the Eleventh Commandment *"Thou Shalt Not Get Caught"*. He knew a bit about getting caught having been a Prisoner of War for a while. If Barney Travers lost his livelihood football seems to have lost a popular character who certainly knew how to score goals as well as how to avoid scoring them. At least when South Shields parted with their best players they received badly needed money for them. Fulham didn't have that consolation.

South Shields 1 Bradford 0:

(inset) the ball on its way into the visitor's net, however, (main photo.') the 'keeper successfully appealed for offside. The club's two main problems are apparent - the empty terraces and the poor pitch.

South Shields action enhanced their status in the football world but did nothing for their popularity with London opponents. Unsurprisingly a convincing defeat ensued at Craven Cottage and - after South Shields had taken maximum points from three games over Easter - a visiting Clapton Orient side *"did the heavy dragoon"* rather too much at Horsley Hill. South Shields beat them away from home the following week and ended this low scoring season in their best position yet of sixth.

****

A little mystery arose following the impressive victory at Sheffield Wednesday on 4 March, when George Keenlyside the longest serving South Shields player and *"one of the finest gentlemen in football"* expressed annoyance when he read in the newspapers that the two goals he had scored were credited to Bill Charlton. Charlton himself did not claim them as, after all, he hadn't even played in the match! All was revealed in the following Saturday's Football Gazette.

Absolving his fellow "scribes" from all blame Wanderer vented his annoyance on a situation centred around Andy Gray a winger who had previously made a couple of appearances for Newcastle United.

Apparently Gray was in business on Tyneside and for some dark reason did not wish it to be known he was away from the district at weekends. Some deception had taken place with the result that completely inaccurate details of the South Shields forward line were published in all newspapers. Noting that Gray's *"consistently good form"* had made him *"well nigh indispensable"* Wanderer concluded that *"it is impossible and if it were possible it would be undesirable, to pretend that Gray is somebody else when the Shieldsmen appear on foreign soil. It cannot be done"*.

In the Football Gazette of 8 April, Wanderer noted that Gray *"has now overcome the difficulty in regard to away matches and in future he will be in a position to turn out for his team whenever he is required."*

(1922/23) A Cup Run

A number of changes were evident as South Shields kicked off the 1922-23 season against newly promoted Southampton before *"a splendid crowd of fully 10,000"*. There was new terracing at the shilling end and the capacity of the ground was now stated at 30,000. The players were clad in their new colours of royal blue shirts and white shorts. The profit of £1,400 which the club had made in the previous season seems modest enough when the transfer fee received for Cresswell is taken into account - let alone those received for Hawes and Woods - but it had allowed a little dabbling in the transfer market. Two new faces that day were Alex Hird, a wing half from Dundee and winger Robert Faulkner, another Scot though he had joined South Shields from Queens Park Rangers after gaining some First Division experience with Blackburn Rovers. The best player that day, however, was veteran George Keenlyside.

A goalless draw was followed by a 2-0 defeat at Notts County. The following Saturday, Ernie Simms scored the club's first two goals of the season at the Dell. This fine victory concluded a highly pleasant visit to Southampton where the South Shields players were entertained to the theatre and shown round the S.S. Aquitania. The long journey home for a match forty eight hours later did no harm as Notts County were beaten by a single goal on Monday evening but then Bury - something of a bogey team - took four points from two matches. Three Counties - Rotherham, Stockport and Derby - were all defeated at Horsley Hill with Bradford City spoiling the sequence with a goalless draw. Gates, however, were falling alarmingly. The attendance for the match against Derby County was estimated as a mere 5,000 albeit on the day South Shields always dreaded – the day Newcastle and Sunderland met at St James's Park.

On 18 November South Shields again became 'The Team That Beat Leeds United' securing a single goal victory at Elland Road.

It will be noted that goals were still in short supply as the offside rule continued to frustrate forwards. The defensive record of South Shields was also due to the presence of tough tackling full backs and especially the splendid goalkeeping of Willis Walker with his much envied ability to save penalties. What a fine purchase he had proved since he was plucked from the ashes of the old Leeds City club three years earlier. A county cricketer who had made his debut for Nottinghamshire against Yorkshire at Dewsbury in 1913 (and was the only player from that summer who lived to see the 1990's), Walker continued to live in Leeds commuting the 100 miles to South Shields only on match days. His training was done at Elland Road so he must have seen the Leeds United players more often than his own team mates.

Walker no doubt had a difficult week after helping South Shields to inflict a home defeat on promotion chasing Leeds United and must have heard some hard words before Leeds gained their revenge with a 2-0 victory in the return match at Horsley Hill a week later. A North Star reporter noted that *"For some reason not apparent to the onlookers he* [Walker] *made no attempt to save the first goal and the ball bounced slowly into the net unchallenged, while the second goal might have been prevented"*. Well, well, well.

Perhaps we shouldn't begrudge a man a peaceful train journey home in the company of his friends/ opponents. A goalkeeper's life is a tough one. In an unseasonal match at Horsley Hill on 23 December Willis Walker had to put up with some harassment from Clapton Orient forward Jack Tonner, who then took time off to *"seemingly"* kick South Shields centre half Hardy for which he was sent off. Dismissals were rare in the twenties but another one followed five minutes later when the South Shields captain Alf Maitland received his marching orders. *"He was seemingly holding Bailey off from harassing Walker and may have kicked him but this was not seen from the press box"* noted the Sunday Sun cautiously.

Clapton Orient were further reduced when Galbraith was injured and the ten men beat the nine men 3-0.

Incidentally the Football Association enquiry into the match found that a caution was sufficient for Maitland but suspended Tonner for a month. Clapton Orient were also warned about crowd hostility towards South Shields in the return match a week later.

The crowd of 18,750 witnessed a goalless draw. The replay at Blackburn on Thursday afternoon provided a surprise victory for South Shields though even the North Eastern papers thought it was a fortunate one. After 14 min-utes Jack Smith accepted a pass from Kccnly-side and drove the ball so hard at the Blackburn goalkeeper, Sewell, that it slipped through his hands. This was the only shot South Shields had in the whole match but it proved sufficient as the

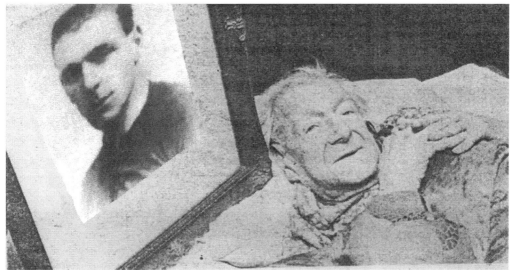

Alf Maitland (who was sold to Middlesbrough for £4,000 in 1923), pictured on the 21st December 1981. In his own words: "*They used to call me Dirty Maitland in those days. Oh aye I was a tough lad then. I played the game clean but if anyone came the rough stuff well.....*" He also recalled that he was once approached by a Fulham player with a bribe to throw a match; "*I reported it to the manager and he told the football league. The player was banned but I was given the bird by the crowd every time I played after that - and all because I was honest.*" Alf sadly died on the 22 December just a few days after this interview.

Crowd estimates were now generally below ten thousand so a Cup run would be welcome and fate obliged for once. Halifax Town from the Third Division (North) were the first round visitors and some interest was shown in two brothers called Hall who had played for South Shields in pre-League days. They were of little help to Halifax with South Shields winning a one sided game 3-1 before a crowd of 10,734.

In the next round First Division Blackburn Rovers were the visitors. There was no counter attraction and - a rarity - special trains ran *from* Newcastle and Sunderland *to* South Shields.

Blackburn forwards were very poor and it certainly pleased the small band of South Shields supporters who had made a tedious journey in wretched weather.

The third round tie was away to Queens Park Rangers but here luck deserted South Shields. For the third year in succession a Third Division (South) club defeated them, this time by 3-0. To rub salt in the wound two of the goals were scored by the same Richard Parker from whom so much had been expected when he arrived at Horsley Hill from Coventry in 1920.

League fare at this time was unexciting although more matches were won than lost. Home crowds remained in four figures, a situation not helped by further strikes locally by miners and dockers. Once again the only high score of the season involved Barnsley - this time it was Barnsley's turn to win 5-0 at Oakwell.

New opponents over Easter were Manchester United who although a famous old club did not possess the charisma they were to acquire later in the century. They proved too strong for South Shields winning 3-0 at both Old Trafford and Horsley Hill. The home defeat was not to the liking of Wanderer whose verdict in the following Saturday's Football Gazette was uncharacteristically vehement. *"I cannot conceive of a more depressing exhibition than that given on Monday against Manchester United. Every department of the team and every individual player seemed to vie with one another in their incompetency and blundering, and if their opponents had routed them by half a dozen goals instead of three no one would have been in the least surprised".* More in this vein followed concluding with the gloomy prediction that relegation would be the prelude to many years of Third Division football.

Relegation! A fate not seriously contemplated before now. If the players read these harsh words after drawing 0-0 with Hull City that afternoon they responded in the best possible manner by taking three points from Crystal Palace and four from Fulham to finish the season in thirteenth position.

* *

A history of South Shields FC in the 1922-23 season would be incomplete without mention of an internal matter. The previous summer the club had appointed Jimmy Lawrence as team manager, a position which was distinct from that already held by Mr Jack Tinn who was general manager and secretary. Jimmy Lawrence had a distinguished career behind him as goalkeeper in Newcastle United's golden era before the war when he had played in five Cup Finals. Latterly he had been chairman of the Players Union. His stay at South Shields was a short one as his position was terminated in January as *"an economy measure"*. The feeling that he had not been treated well by the club resulted in a number of letters to the Shields Daily Gazette culminating in one from himself. In this letter he stated that although he remained on good terms with all individuals at the club and wished the team well he was disappointed that his suggestions regarding training were not adopted and was unhappy at being required to spend Saturday afternoons away from the club watching other players. In view of these grievances the request that he take a reduction in salary of £1 a week had made the parting of the ways inevitable. He thanked the numerous people who had written to the press supporting him.

Further sympathy for Mr Lawrence (who had since been appointed manager of Preston North End) was expressed at the founding meeting of the South Shields Supporters Club in April, which filled a local hall to overflowing.

In June it was announced that South Shields Football Club had made a loss of £4,990-17-0.

(1923/24) Table Toppers Again

An even stranger name than South Shields would be opposing famous name clubs in the Second Division in 1923-24. Nelson had won the championship of the Third Division (North) and although they were widely expected to be relegated (and were) this small town team from North Lancashire were not disgraced and their few victories included a single goal victory at Old Trafford and, astonishingly, a 3-1 triumph over champions Leeds United on the last day of the season.

For South Shields the 1923-24 season began with a visit to Fulham as had the inaugural 1919-20 season. Links with that first side had been broken with the departure of the last two survivors in the summer. Alf Maitland took a step up to the First Division with Middlesbrough whilst the ageing George Keenlyside opted to eke out his last season or so with Third Division Hartlepools United. New players included forwards Thomas Brown from Bristol City and Robert Bolam from Darlington. The latter had some First Division experience with Sheffield United.

The Captains toss-up at Craven Cottage before the Fulham match.

Hours before the kick-off at Craven Cottage South Shields seemed to be in trouble. Half backs Hird and Hutchison were stricken down with illness at the team's hotel on the morning of the match and Hird was kept in bed under doctor's orders.
Hasty arrangements were made to register trainer George Lillycrop who had not played for two years, but he was not needed as Hutchison declared himself fit to play, although he was largely a "passenger". Despite these handicaps South Shields got off to a cracking start with a 3-2 victory through goals from Hetherington (2) and Simms.

The two invalids had recovered by Monday and played in a 1-0 home victory over Blackpool. Fulham were again beaten this time 1-0.

After a draw at Blackpool another home victory ensued over Barnsley by 2-0 where the crowd was estimated as being "close upon 10,000".

The first defeat occurred at Barnsley by a single goal, then Manchester United came to Horsley Hill. This turned out to be a most unpleasant encounter. The Sunday Sun noted that the visitors' "ruthless" tactics caused the "lightweight Shieldsmen" to be "buffeted unmercifully". Nobody could remember a Horsley Hill crowd being so openly hostile to a visiting combination.... "the [South Shields] trainer was in frequent demand and it is to be regretted that the referee did not see all that occurred, otherwise those guilty of attempted kicking at each other - and they were not all in the Manchester ranks - would have received their marching orders".

31

Ernie Simms scored the only goal of the game and Willis Walker saved a penalty.

Points were shared at Old Trafford a week later and then the second double of the season was achieved at the expense of Bury. For four weeks South Shields had again topped the Second Division table. The Sunday Sun had enthused about the early victories but after the home win over Bury adopted a more critical stance. *"The enviable position they occupy in the League both delights and surprises their supporters who are not yet accustomed to such glory... it must be acknowledged that many displays such as the Seasiders gave yesterday will soon see them overcome and deposed. They won but their victory was one of the least convincing of the season".*

Cartoon comments regarding the home victory over Bury in October.

And so it proved. The same paper reporting on the 3-0 defeat at Clapton Orient a week later described South Shields as being *"hopelessly out of the picture... shooting weak in the extreme"*. After this match they dropped to fourth position and never rose any higher. Leicester City took four points from them in December and in losing 4-1 at Filbert Street South Shields probably did not impress Mr Winston Churchill who was present.

A remarkable North Eastern League result occurred at Horsley Hill on Boxing Day when South Shields reserves beat Newcastle United reserves 9-0. This League was dominated by the reserve sides of Newcastle, Sunderland and Middlesbrough all of whom were more accustomed to winning matches by such margins. Unusually high scores over Christmas and New Year were often regarded with suspicion.... but they will have to remain suspicions.

(The breathalyser had not been invented then). Goals generally were a little more plentiful than they had been for a couple of years despite the sterling defensive work which had been responsible for South Shields' earlier success. On New Years Day there was a 3-3 draw with Port Vale (who fielded a pre-League South Shields favourite Arthur Bridgett) then a creditable victory over high flying Leeds United. An early exit from the FA Cup followed but South Shields put up a plucky performance in losing 3-2 at First Division Burnley.

Well over three years had elapsed since any side had scored six in a South Shields League match but on 19 January that was the number they conceded at Derby - the first time they had let in so many. A double over little Nelson was followed by no points from two games with Hull City.

After losing narrowly at Leeds a single goal was enough to take three points from Stoke who had now almost doubled the length of their name by adding "City".

There was another heavy defeat at Sheffield Wednesday and an entertaining 4-2 victory over Coventry City before the season petered out with a series of low scoring games. The Sunday Sun report of the home game with Bristol City deserves anthologising so is reproduced here. South Shields ended the season in ninth position.

* *

So after another season in which South Shields had led the Second Division table for some weeks the question should be asked "Was promotion ever on?" Not on your life it wasn't. Many faithful supporters who could remember the similar situation in 1920 must have noticed that there was rather more elbow room now than there was in the year of "the usual twenty thousand".

A remarkable statistic from late in the season puts the limited potential of the club into stark perspective. On Good Friday a South Shields team did play before 20,000 but they were the reserves playing the match which decided the North Eastern League championship - a 1-1 draw with Newcastle United reserves at St James's Park. The team they weren't good enough to get into was entertaining Bradford City before half that number at Horsley Hill. Small consolation that South Shields reserves won the championship of their League.

Four years of Second Division football had provided much entertainment and interest to the people of an impoverished district in hungry times, but where was Warney Cresswell now? Or Alf Maitland? The most fervent South Shields supporter knew in his heart that the famous visitors, the Sheffield Wednesdays, Nottingham Forests and Manchester Uniteds were all "down on their luck" when they called at Horsley Hill and that they would eventually return to where they belonged. All that remained for South Shields was avoiding relegation. Still that had not been a problem up to now. Perhaps it could be staved off indfinitely.

FOOTBALL AT ITS WORS

Not a Thrill in Shields Encounter.

POINTS DIVIDED.

South Shields rung down the Second League curtain ... Horsley Hill with a miserable dr of one goal each with Bristol City, the bott team in the competition.

Evidence of the departed interest in t local club's doings for the present season r reflected in the small attendance of spec tors, there not being more than a coupl thousand at the most.

The weather was bad, and the footb worse, neither team doing anything enthusng about. Guyan set the ball roll against the wind in a pelting rain that soon to damp the ardour of the players. The op ing play was scrappy, indeed, and when af a quarter of an hour some weak defens work on the part of the home team snub Smailes, the Bristol centre-half, to put p Walker at close quarters the home cro applauded sarcastically.

Shields rallied somewhat after this reve and made things hum in the visitors' l division, but the home forwards were pe fully weak in front of goal, added to wh Vallis gave a crisp display between visitors' sticks. He got some awkward sh away from Guyan and Smith, and tw cleared beautifully-placed corners by Bro

How Shields Equalised.

Matthewson got past on the Shields rig and eventually forced a corner off Dyer. T the former placed well; the ball came again, but Brown on the left, with a qu first time drive equalised for Shields. shot hit the underside of the cross bar, ball glancing into the net.

There were those who expected Shields run away with the game in the second h but such were doomed to disappointme for there was no more scoring. In the aggi gate the visitors had equally as much of attack to their credit as Shields, and the closing stages of the game came wit an aire of annexing both points.

A couple of marvellous saves by Wal in the home goal, however, saved the sit tion.

Naturally South Shields' supporters wondering what will happen in the ret match at Bristol next Saturday, the f one of the season.

SOUTH SHIELDS:--Walker, Ridley, Robson, Wi Nicholson, Metcalf; Matthewson, Smith, Guyan, Th son, Brown.

BRISTOL CITY:--Vallis; Hughes, Dyer; Hall, Sm Torrance; Nimble, Mays, Walsh, Sutherland, Pocock. Referee:--Mr. T. Hall.

Don't believe a word of it! This reporter was sulking because he hadn't been sent to Wembley to cover the Newcastle v. Aston Villa Cup Final. The rain didn't prevent crowds from gathering outside Newcastle newspaper offices to be kept up to date with the latest score.

(1924/25) A Jekyll And Hyde Season

In 1924 the Football League abandoned its policy of pairing clubs to meet on successive Saturdays and nobody was sorry. South Shields began their season with two home games but lost both, first to newly promoted Portsmouth and then Blackpool. Midweek opponents still came round again quickly and, after drawing at Fulham, South Shields lost 5-0 at Blackpool whose prolific centre forward Harry Bedford scored four. Not a happy start for South Shields but talk of disaster would be inappropriate. A Blackpool newspaper reported that after the match a heap of rubbish under the stand at Bloomfield Road was found to be on fire and quickly extinguished. Football history is studded with references to fires in stands and a true disaster was forever waiting to happen.

It was to wait another sixty years before finally happening at Bradford City.

The press enthused about the match on 13 September with references to *"hurricane shooting"* as Wolverhampton Wanderers drew 3-3 at Horsley Hill. Centre half Cyril Hunter, newly signed from Brentford and destined for distinction of a sort, made an impressive debut. This match was followed by another wearisome run of eleven games in which neither side scored more than once. The authorities were aware of the problem, which must have been having a detrimental effect on attendances generally. A remedy was not far away. There was a good attendance on 27 September when Middlesbrough paid their first League visit.

Shields' 'keeper Walker in action at Fulham: September 1924.

The visitors brought a large contingent with them. A former South Shields player called William Hick, who had never got into the first team at Horsley Hill, scored Middlesbrough's winning goal in a match played in a cup tie atmosphere. The first South Shields victory occurred in the ninth match against Bradford City.

There were plenty of goals in a light-hearted meeting with Scottish friends Dundee on 29 October. This was the benefit match for Willis Walker. South Shields won 6-5 but there was a poor turn out which the local press thought might have been due to the imminence of the General Election.

Walker's long stay at South Shields was ending and he played his last match against Crystal Palace on 8 November, finding more convenient employment guarding the Bradford net. In 195 appearances he had kept a clean sheet on no fewer than 74 occasions and the club must have been sorry to part with him.

Well into December South Shields alternated between 21st and 22nd position, but press reports were quite encouraging and there was a feeling that they were unlucky. On the morning of 20 December they had only won once in eighteen attempts but the 4-0 victory over Stoke City that afternoon signalled the start of a remarkable recovery.

Victory at Coventry City on Christmas Day was followed by a narrow defeat at Portsmouth then another victory over Coventry by 4-1 on New Years Day. A 2-1 defeat at Crystal Palace in the FA Cup drew an unsolicited tribute from a Palace supporter. *"It was one of the best exhibitions seen at Selhurst this season and I can hardly credit your position in the League".*

The corner had been turned. After a 5-2 victory over Barnsley (a result seen before) the last eighteen games of the season brought only three defeats - an astonishing transformation from the first eighteen which had brought only one victory. Far from being relegated, as had been feared, the club finished in their more or less customary position of ninth.

Nor did the scarcity of goals in the last few games detract from the excitement. On 1 April Hull City were *"outclassed and outplayed"* at Horsley Hill and this is how Wanderer reported the 1-0 victory over promotion chasing Derby County on Good Friday.

"The game at Horsley Hill yesterday will live in the memories of all who witnessed it. It was the most thrilling encounter seen on the South Shields ground this season and if it had been a Cup Final the excitement could not have been more intense. When Norman Thompson registered the winning goal there was an extraordinary demonstration and thereafter every movement of the game was followed with the keenest interest. South Shields fully deserved their splendid victory for, after a somewhat disappointing opening they took complete charge of the game after the interval and with ordinary luck would have substantially increased their lead. In spite of the importance of the issue and the robust tactics adopted by both sides the game was wonderfully free from fouls.... There was a record crowd of over 20,000".

So there was life in the old club yet. The poor showing earlier in the season must have been at least partially due to "absence of ordinary luck". This returned a few days later when heavy rain robbed South Shields of another big gate as League leaders Leicester City were held 1-1 on a Horsley Hill quagmire.

(1925/26) An Enjoyable Season

1925 saw three changes in the football world, two significant and one momentous. The seeding system for the FA Cup was altered although this chiefly affected Third Division clubs who were now exempt until the first round proper as distinct from previously when some had to play in preliminary rounds. Survivors joined First and Second Division clubs in what now became the third round.

The Football League now allowed official attendance figures to be published for each match so that newspapers no longer had to rely on estimated figures, which often varied considerably.

Important though these changes were they pale into insignificance when compared to the change in the offside law. The number of goals scored in the 1925-26 season was a sharp increase on the previous season now that it was no longer possible for full backs to employ the blatant spoiling tactics which had so annoyed the crowd at the South Shields v West Ham United match four years earlier.

Swansea Town had been promoted from the Third Division (South) and - like Southampton and Portsmouth before them - their first game in higher company was against South Shields, this time at the Vetch Field. Two goals by long serving centre forward Jack Oxberry gave South Shields a welcome opening day victory though they represented his only contribution to the season as he was seriously injured in the home match against Sheffield Wednesday a week later and was unable to resume for a year.

Another popular centre forward George Guyan scored twice against Wolves but the next time a hat trick was scored in a match concerning South Shields it was by an opponent - ironically Ernie Simms. Simms had been a prolific scorer for Luton Town both before and after the war but when he returned to his native North East he

proved something of a disappointment and had been allowed to go to Stockport County. There too his record was unsensational despite having toured Australia with a Football Association XI. Confronted by his old team mates at Edgeley Park on 26 September he suddenly rediscovered his old form and scored a hat trick in the first twenty minutes. Stockport won 4-1.

A good run followed with home wins of 5-2 v Fulham and 5-1 v Portsmouth separated by away victories over Hull City and Clapton Orient and a goalless draw with Chelsea. (The Monday afternoon victory over Portsmouth concluded an unproductive Northern tour for the visitors who had lost 7-1 at Darlington forty-eight hours earlier).

In keeping with the unpredictability of football no points at all were gained from the next four games, with Blackpool and Bradford City both winning at Horsley Hill. The Blackpool match was another thriller with South Shields twice taking the lead only to lose 4-3.

The Christmas and New Year holiday period was to be the most enjoyable and arguably the most successful spell in the club's League history. Preston North End had been spending large sums of money recruiting Scottish players and the acquisition of two more just before Christmas must have ensured a home victory on Boxing Day. After all they were unbeaten at Deepdale and the opposition was only poverty stricken little South Shields. For a change let's hear what the opposition press had to say. The Lancashire Daily Post reported:

"There was to be a killing at Deepdale on Saturday and over thirty thousand people assembled to be in at the death but something went wrong with the programme. The corpse was there certainly but it was not the right one. It was Goliath's not David's.....it was a question of adaptability to conditions and of sounder field strategy such as South Shields possessed".

After criticising Preston the report continues *".... by comparison South Shields were always a combined and compact force, alert, full of endurance and capacity, moving in a body in the same direction and capable of getting the maximum from the minimum of effort. Better football on such a ground indeed one could not wish to see. It was a triumph of brains as well as industry.*

"They were flattered a trifle by the margin of their success perhaps, for one of their goals should not have stood, but nobody would wish to question their right to a handsome victory. It is a long time since I saw the ball on a greasy ground more effectively and accurately used by first time touching and placing without frills. Moreover the men kept their feet better in the slush".

High praise indeed as South Shields romped to a 4-0 victory with goals from Thirlaway, Smith and Parker (2). To prove it was no mere flash in the pan they travelled to Middlesbrough on New Years Day and won 2-1. Richard Parker scoring both in a victory which must have done wonders for their status in the North East. (It should be pointed out that this Richard Parker is not the same man who was signed from Coventry in 1920).

Completion of the double over Swansea Town must have seemed small beer while progress to the next stage of the FA Cup involved a hollow victory over a Northern Alliance side. A newspaper observed wryly that this stage (now the third round) could not have provided less tempting fare with Newcastle United, Sunderland and South Shields all drawn at home to Aberdare Athletic, Boston United and Chilton Colliery.

The anticipated home victories materialised by 4-1, 8-1 and 3-0 respectively. The Durham miners who opposed South Shields had reached that stage impressively with victories over Rochdale of the Third Division and Carlisle United (still a North Eastern League club).

Though few people ever heard of Chilton Colliery FC before or since, the magic of the FA Cup held sway and the Horsley Hill crowd of 14,866 who saw them lose gamely exceeded that for any League match that season against famous clubs like Chelsea or Wolverhampton Wanderers. First Division Birmingham were drawn to play at Horsley Hill in the next round and they suggested that the match should be played at either Newcastle or Sunderland where, not only would the attendance be much bigger, but their own travelling supporters would be in less danger of being locked out. Perhaps the other old problem made the switch desirable. Reporting the 5-1 victory over Stoke City on 23 January the Football Gazette said that *"the players had frequently to wade through pools of water which converted the West end of the field into something like a quagmire".* South Shields declined to switch - a decision much applauded locally - and prepared for one of the biggest matches in their history.

The great day arrived. Unsold tickets returned from Birmingham had sold like hot cakes. With no counter attraction crowds flocked into the town. The South Shields Tramways Department did the town proud with no fewer than 42 tramcars to take people to the ground. The crowd was in fact in the region of 17,000 and it seems likely that fears of an excessively high gate kept some people away. The match was no classic but worth seeing. Defences dominated with South Shields employing spoiling tactics very effectively.

After 18 minutes Jack Smith put South Shields ahead with a shot from close range. Birmingham's forwards seldom got past the South Shields full backs but on one such occasion left back Mick Ridley locked his arms round the Birmingham centre forward Joe Bradford who scored with the resultant penalty. Towards the end of the game Alex Trotter's first time shot rebounded off Birmingham goalkeeper Tremelling and Trotter's second chance was enough to put South Shields into the next round.

The excitement engendered by the Cup-tie evaporated almost immediately and the crowd for the 4-2 victory over Stockport County a week later was under 7,000. In the next round of the Cup South Shields proved no match for Bolton Wanderers who beat them 3-0 at Burnden Park and went on to win the cup. The share of a gate of more than 48,000 was very welcome but the club could still not resist offers for players such as that which took full back Laurie Crown to Newcastle United in early March.

South Shields played a goalless draw before another large crowd at Chelsea but this only emphasised the gulf between richer and poorer clubs. Darlington's visit on 20 March was awaited with interest, and nostalgia was expressed for the days when the two clubs had vied for prominence in the North Eastern League. Darlington proved to be no sentimentalists adding a 4-2 victory to their 4-1 success at Feethams earlier in the season. In fact South Shields dealings with Darlington were to yield precious little reward in the years ahead.

The problem facing all clubs - the midweek afternoon match - resurfaced when Clapton Orient, whose previous visits had been lively affairs, came to Horsley Hill.

Few supporters who were in employment would risk absenting themselves for such a match and those without work couldn't afford to go anyway. A derisory 2,797 witnessed a 1-0 home victory.

The other North Eastern club in the Second Division was of course Middlesbrough, a much greater draw than Darlington, and with memories of the New Years Day victory at Ayresome Park still fresh in the memory, the biggest League crowd of the season -14,839 - saw the two clubs draw 2-2 on Good Friday. This proved to be the last time a five figure crowd ever assembled for a League match at Horsley Hill.

Times were hard in South Shields as elsewhere. There had been a bitter strike by seamen earlier in the season and now the miners who formed a large section of the local workforce were facing a desperate crisis as their employers "offered" to reduce their already low wages.

As the week began in which events moved towards the General Strike in support of the miners, South Shields played their last game of the season. Many a local man with much else to worry about must have decided that a shilling could not be spared at Horsley Hill. 3,027 people saw Port Vale defeated in a match described as *"dull and uninteresting"*.

(1926/27) More Downs Than Ups, Another Cup Run And Mayhem At Middlesbrough.

"The South Shields forwards as a whole lacked cohesion and understanding and their efforts were frequently scrappy and disjointed.... it was in front of goal that their greatest weakness was revealed.... Having regard to the obvious weakness of the inside forwards.... I think the directors would have been advised to have made some change.... I have no doubt if there has been no improvement.... they will take immediate steps to remedy the defects."

Wanderer (at his rattiest)
Shields Football Gazette, 27 November 1926.

The captains shake hands before the match at Hull in August.

It might be pointed out as a postscript that this tirade refers to the previous week's match against Barnsley, which this ineffective bunch had managed to win by seven goals to one.

****

Notts County, newly relegated with Manchester City, opened the season at Horsley Hill. South Shields won 5-0 causing local reporters to wonder what County had been doing in the First Division at all. This bright start proved illusory with only one point from the next six games. This single point might not have been theirs had Middlesbrough (pointless after three games) decided to play the as yet little known George Camsell when they visited Horsley Hill on 11 September. The result was a goalless draw. Middlesbrough gave Camsell a chance in their next match and he proceeded to create a new Football League record by scoring 59 goals in the season.

The attendance for the Middlesbrough match at 7,519 was little more than half of that for the Good Friday match between the same clubs five months earlier. There was little money about, the miners had yet to return to work for their new (reduced) rates of pay and the short League

history of South Shields FC had seen attendances fall from being fifth highest in the Second Division in 1919-20 to being the lowest in 1925-26. Significantly Mr Jack Tinn who had been secretary/ manager since North Eastern League days was looking elsewhere and had accepted a position with Oldham Athletic. South Shields did not wish to lose him and Oldham agreed to hold the matter in abeyance.

South Shields 5 Chelsea 1. Even this far into the story that scoreline has a strange look to it and an odd game it was. For a start both goalkeepers were called McKenna. *"Practically a hurricane"* blew throughout the match. Metcalf opened the scoring in the first minute and Jack Oxberry, recently returned after a year on the injury list, scored another in the fourth minute. At ten minutes it was 3-0. A goal scored directly by a player taking a corner is an event of great rarity but Matthewson managed it with a powerful shot which the *"hurricane"* diverted into the net for him. The wind was equally obliging just before half time when Matthewson repeated his profitable action.

In the second half the wind favoured Chelsea but their consolation goal was neutralised by a penalty converted by Ridley. Matthewson's two gale force goals must have been followed by a painful second half because when the players were leaving the field he made the belated suggestion to the visitors that they should *"play the game"*. Chelsea centre forward Turnbull objected to this remark and capped an eventful afternoon by striking the South Shields winger. This was witnessed by a linesman and earned Turnbull a two month suspension.

Victories remained scarce although Grimsby Town were beaten a fortnight later. On 20 November came the big win over Barnsley about which the Football Gazette reporter saw so little to enthuse. The representative of the Sunday Sun was equally unimpressed, heaping scorn on the *"week display"* of centre forward Oxberry whose failure to score had robbed South Shields of the chance of double figures. He was more generous to the Barnsley goalkeeper, Carrigan, who *"played a splendid game"*.

Were they just being perverse in the press box that afternoon? Nobody carped a week later when South Shields recorded a fine win over Manchester City at Maine Road. A 1-0 victory at home to struggling Darlington may not seem a very great achievement but this proved to be the only time South Shields won a League match against that club.

Real life continued to impinge. A letter writer said he was surprised that South Shields gates were as high as they were *"when one takes into consideration the fact, which is perhaps news to you, that a resolution was passed calling upon the miners not to support the local football club for refusing a collection in aid of the miners children during the coal stoppage"*. This "fact" was immediately refuted not by the club but by the editor of the Shields Daily Gazette who pointed out that collections for miners' dependents were taking place at home matches and that the club had issued free passes to six collectors. The collecting secretary of the women's committee wrote to say that the club had been most co-operative but that collections taken at two matches had met with such meagre results that they had been abandoned.

The club was now experiencing something of a revival. Their sixth consecutive match without defeat took place on Christmas Day when Preston North End shared the points before the highest crowd of the season so far. A visit to Deepdale two days later saw the previous year's 4-0 result reversed but that did not prevent another comparatively high crowd on New Years Day. Old friends Hull City were the visitors and they brought about a thousand supporters by special train. The former South Shields centre forward George Guyan was cheered when he took the field and again when he scored Hull's consolation in a match which South Shields won 3-1.

The draw for the FA Cup had given South Shields a home draw against Plymouth Argyle. It must be unusual for a Third Division club to ask Second Division opponents to sell ground rights but this is what Plymouth suggested pointing out that there would be a much higher attendance if the match was switched to Home Park. South Shields declined the offer and the match took place at Horsley Hill on 8 January.

On Friday evening a special train left Plymouth for this longest of journeys with about 500 people on board but many of them disembarked at York, Stockton, West Hartlepool, Sunder-land and Newcastle. In an age when long distance travel was a rare luxury many Northerners exiled in Devon and Cornwall were clearly taking advantage of a cheap football excursion to visit seldom seen relatives - an illustration of football serving a larger section of the community than usual. About 120 Argyle enthusiasts stayed the course and were met by drab weather at 6.45am. The long hours must have dragged by for these travel-stained Westcountrymen.

The game itself provided South Shields with a victory by three goals to one, the scorers being Hunter, Oxberry and Jack Smith. The Horsley Hill pitch was up to its usual wet weather standard and the greatest roar of the afternoon came when a Plymouth player failed to score from a hotly disputed penalty. The victory caused much satisfaction locally though it is galling to read in a book published in the 1990's of "facts" about Plymouth Argyle that this Cup-tie was one of two occasions when Argyle were knocked out by a non-League side!

The attendance of 9,811 paying £696 would have been higher were it not for the weather. Also Newcastle were also playing at home to Notts County. It will be recalled that County had failed to impress when losing 5-0 at Horsley Hill on the opening day. They did even worse that day losing 8-1 at St James's Park but they still managed to defeat South Shields 4-1 at Meadow Lane a week later. Sheffield Wednesday were the next cup tie opponents at Hillsborough, and the South Shields players spent three days training at Matlock in Derbyshire.

The change of air proved beneficial as the First Division opponents were held to a 1-1 draw. The South Shields goal was scored by Tom Matthewson which must have been doubly satisfying as he had been rejected by Wednesday earlier in his career. South Shields defended resolutely for most of the game with young reserve goalkeeper Taylor being the hero of the match whilst full backs Wilson and Phizacklea also merited praise.

Wednesday saw Wednesday at Horsley Hill bringing 1,500 supporters on a day with *"scenes reminiscent of a Bank Holiday in South Shields"*. Thousands more came from Newcastle and Sunderland. Some of their employers must have wondered where they were or perhaps spotted them in the crowd. Community singing was led by Marsden Colliery Band and a new record crowd of 23,266, paying £1,837-1-0, saw South Shields triumph by the only goal of the match scored by Jack Smith. A memorable afternoon but South Shields would never win another Cup-tie.

The League season had been an indifferent one but even a 6-2 defeat at Southampton was forgotten when Swansea Town came to Horsley Hill for the next round. There were no visiting supporters this time but, even in the absence of Welshmen, the community singing passed off enjoyably as the attendance record was broken for the last and final time. But the 24,348 who paid £1,888 saw Swansea score in the second minute and go further ahead in the seventh. Jack Smith pulled one back for South Shields two minutes later and the home side attacked relentlessly before Trotter equalised in a robust match of many fouls. In Wales in midweek, Swansea again scored two early goals but this time South Shields could only reply once.

Not many football fans were ever much convinced by the old cliché following an FA Cup defeat of "at least we can now concentrate on the League", but League form was deteriorating from indifferent to desperate. How many supporters did South Shields have anyway? The League match against Bradford City postponed ten days by the Swansea Cup-ties was watched by 2,976.

When old friends Fulham managed to wrest a point from South Shields for the first time in eight visits, the crowd of 4,296 caused the Shields Daily Gazette to confront its readers with some indisputable truths. *"What a difference that defeat at Swansea made to South Shields prospects for the rest of the season. But for that lapse Shields would have been Cup mad on Saturday, whereas a stranger to the town would never have imagined that there was a match at Horsley Hill at all, so little was the interest that it aroused. Football supporters are a fickle lot, and no wonder Shields have to adopt the undignified role of nursing team supplying the needs of others and at the same time augmenting their funds to counter balance the shortcomings of their followers"*.

And that was before the 5-0 defeat by Middlesbrough at Ayresome Park, before two consecutive 6-1 defeats at Barnsley and Blackpool, before (worst of all) the short journey to Darlington on 23 April where "whilst the Shieldsmen contented themselves with overindulgence in pattern weaving Darlington took the game seriously and their motto was to get there". Darlington got there eight times with their centre forward, the eminent-ly punnable Ruddy scoring five of them.

Could any crumbs of comfort be found from this appalling run? Some could. Goalkeeper Alan Taylor saved a penalty at Ayresome Park which meant that George Camsell had to be content with his fourth hat trick of the season instead of his fourth four (and there had been a five). An undefeated run of fourteen games at Horsley Hill was only ended by Wolves in the last match and promotion-chasing teams returned home with little reward. Manchester City only took one point from South Shields all season and their failure to win at Horsley Hill on 16 April kept them in the Second Division because of Portsmouth's wafer thin goal average superiority. The only South Shields victory in the last ten matches came in a bad tempered game against promoted Portsmouth. (The team that scored eight against them was relegated).

Only three points and two places separated South Shields from relegation. Days when they had topped the table and drawn crowds of twenty thousand for League matches were now a fading memory. Nobody needed a crystal ball to see where the club was heading.

Before leaving this season of high scores for and against, of Cup excitement and League ineptitude, it is necessary to look again at that match at Ayresome Park. A series of headlines in the following day's Northern Echo read:

'AFTER THE BATTLE: MIDDLESBROUGH DRESSING ROOM LIKE AN AMBULANCE STATION'

'COUNTING THE COST OF VICTORY'

'PEASE OUT OF ACTION FOR SEASON: CAMSELL CARRIES ON WITH BROKEN THUMB'

'MARCHING ORDERS FOR SOUTH SHIELD PIVOT'

Perhaps it would be best to let the Middlesbrough reporter of that newspaper tell us about that violent Wednesday.

"The Middlesbrough dressing room was like a field ambulance station after this match at Ayresome Park last evening.... Pease, his left collar bone broken, was slung up awaiting delivery to the doctors' shop sad at the thought that he had kicked his last as far as this season's football is concerned. Camsell was being helped into his clothes with what had every suggestion of being a broken right thumb and Miller was lying on the massage table dazed and groaning.

"The man who had done it all, Hunter the South Shields centre half, was in a neighbouring room humiliated not half enough by his dismissal from the field ten minutes before the end.

"All through the contest Hunter's was the influence which was threatening to spoil the contest, and it was a tragedy from a Middlesbrough point of view that instead of cautioning him, the referee [Mr A Scholey of Sheffield] *did not deem it wise to point him to the line side at an earlier stage."*

"The game was young when Camsell turned a ball to Williams and Hunter made sure that the Middlesbrough leader took no further part in that particular movement. Camsell picked himself up, wrung his hand repeatedly, but did not retire though apparently in considerable pain....

"Ten minutes of the second half had gone when Pease, essaying a grand 25 yard left foot drive, was downed by Hunter. The Middlesbrough man was assisted off, and took no further part in the game. Although it was evident from the way Hunter tore across the field that he meant to stop Pease, there was not the vice in the tackle that was patent when he felled Miller in the penalty area.

"The referee ordered Hunter to the dressing room, and he slunk off the field, I know, to the cries of execration even from Shields supporters. And as he left Camsell failed with the penalty which followed Hunter's last and most glaring indiscretion.... As a result of the heavy chapter of injuries - they cannot be described as accidents.... it was reported from Ayresome Park last night that Pease has an oblique fracture of the collar bone, that Camsell has a chip off the bone at the joint of the right thumb, and that Miller is suffering from concussion."

So here was an occasion when a South Shields player made an impression. When the reserve sides of these clubs met at the same ground a week later in the North Eastern League it was noticeable that Middlesbrough declined to field any player who might be needed for a forthcoming promotion clash at Portsmouth. Once bitten twice shy, though the Northern Echo reporter was at pains to point out that Cyril Hunter's display was a one man circus act and absolved the rest of the team from any blame.

Whilst the Battle of Ayresome Park saw a Camsell hat trick which took his goal tally to fifty for the season and saw Middlesbrough surpass their record number of goals it also resulted in the longest suspension yet imposed for misconduct on the field. Early in April, Hunter was banned until the end of November.

(1927/28) The Team That Did Not Beat Leeds United

(or Barnsley, Blackpool, Bristol City, Clapton Orient, Grimsby Town, Manchester City, Nottingham Forest, Notts County, Oldham Athletic, Preston North End, Reading, Stoke City, West Bromwich Albion or Wolverhampton Wanderers).

Portsmouth resented their defeat at Horsley Hill in April but this had proved to be merely a stumbling block on their path to promotion and by the time the new season began their dealings with South Shields had proved much more beneficial. They had secured the services of Jack Tinn as manager and in later years he was to experience the highest honours in English football at a time when his former club was only a memory. His new team began their First Division career at nearby Roker Park which gave Mr Tinn the opportunity to visit South Shields in the evening, when his many years of service to the club were recalled at a large gathering and he was presented with golf clubs, a gold ring and various other gifts. South Shields had advertised for a new manager but after considering twenty nine applicants had decided to fill the position from within their own ranks and appointed director Ernest E. Douglass.

A new arrival was goalkeeper Peter Shevlin who had played in two Scottish Cup Finals for Celtic and had a winners medal from one of them. He was in for a busy season. The party for Mr Tinn on the evening of 27 August was overshadowed by the 5-1 home defeat by Leeds United that afternoon. All six goals had been scored in the second half and the only consolation had been the attendance figure of 9,826.

Once again the players spent a few days at Matlock between two matches in the Midlands but if any benefit accrued it was only that their stay began with a heavy defeat at Nottingham Forest and ended with a narrow one at Wolverhampton. They seem to have been unlucky at Molineux where Shevlin *"displayed the coolness of a veteran"* (which he was). Full back J.G. Ridley had been transferred to Manchester City and he made his debut for his new club at Horsley Hill in a match which City won 1-0. The first point came in the fifth game (2-2 at home to Wolves) and it was enough to put South Shields ahead of four pointless rivals. Not quite the highlight of the season but certainly their highest League position. Matches against Hull and Preston gave cause for optimism that the corner had been turned and that defeats might now only be single goal affairs. But at Swansea on 1 October Jack Oxberry joined the unhappy band of players who finished on the losing side, despite scoring a hat trick, with the home team scoring six.

Good humour prevailed and when a victory finally came against Fulham on 8 October, Wanderer overheard a man on a tramcar mocking those who had gone to Sunderland and wondering why they didn't stay at home and watch a winning team. To the delight of the eavesdropping journalist the man added that he was looking forward to reading what Wanderer had to say about the match.

Some comfort was drawn a week later when South Shields made an odd contribution to football's statistical history. By drawing 0-0 at Oakwell they ended Barnsley's record breaking run of scoring in 43 consecutive League games. It must be owned that Barnsley's achievement was rather academic. It had failed to lift them above mid table and the run included occasions when they had scored the merest consolation as at Horsley Hill the previous November and also a 9-1 defeat at Molineux. Be that as it may the notoriously leaky South Shields defence was the first that Barnsley had failed to pierce in more than a year, a fact not lost on the local press. The record, to date, has only been beaten once (by Chesterfield who scored in 46 consecutive matches in 1929 and 1930) and equalled once (by First Division Manchester City in 1937-38).

A point was extracted from Oldham at Boundary Park and after a home defeat by Notts County a true cause for celebration occurred, though it was far away at Southampton. In the early stages South Shields seemed indecisive especially in defence and Southampton's first goal seemed overdue at twenty-five minutes after they had twice hit the woodwork. South Shields' equaliser was something of a freak goal when a shot from Henderson rebounded off the foot of a Southampton defender into and out of the arms of ex-Sunderland goalkeeper Allen. Just before the interval Jack Oxberry attempted a long powerful shot and succeeded in giving South Shields the lead. The same player scored again immediately after the break and although Southampton managed to reduce the deficit South Shields dominated the rest of the game, Scott and Jack Smith adding further goals with South Shields eventually winning 5-3. Unquestionably this fine performance was the only highlight in a dreadful season. What a shame that few if any South Shields supporters would have been present.

Nobody could begrudge South Shields the glory of this one dramatic achievement. Wanderer was ecstatic. *"It was a famous victory"* he began before quoting complimentary reports from national newspapers. His observation that the team performed better away from home brought forth a letter from "Old Player" who laid the blame partly on barrackers in the North Stand. Predictably a home defeat by Grimsby Town followed.

Reading were now the only club below South Shields in the table. They solved that problem by beating South Shields 5-1 at Elm Park, but Wanderer was still in good spirits and dismissed those who were resigned to relegation as *"super pessimists"*. Perhaps he was wandering, though he would doubtless recall the dramatic recovery of 1924-25.

One Southampton swallow didn't make a summer and most of the winter would be over before South Shields recorded another victory.

Twenty-second position had now been reached and was not vacated. Cyril Hunter's long suspension ended but his recall to the team for the visit to Stamford Bridge did nothing to prevent a 6-0 defeat. A home draw against Blackpool preceded eight successive defeats. Jack Tinn, who had spent so many years lamenting the necessity of parting with players, visited at the end of the year and took Jack Smith back to Portsmouth with him. Smith proceeded to score 11 goals in 18 First Division games to add to the paltry 4 he had scored for South Shields in 18 Second Division outings.

Even the FA Cup seemed to be losing its appeal, the visit to Middlesbrough being more trouble than it was worth. Although a healthy number of the dwindling band of regulars made the trip, the 3-0 defeat was about as much as anybody had expected. Sadly there was a renewal of the bad blood between these clubs and after a first half of *"Cup-tie vigour"* the second half began with *"an epidemic of fouls"*. South Shields inside forward Stevenson was sent off for taking a Middlesbrough player *"off his feet"*.

The referee called both sides together for a lecture but fouls continued and ten minutes from the end a second South Shields player, Henderson, received his marching orders for tripping an opponent. Since North Eastern League days South Shields had been on the most cordial terms with the Middlesbrough club but, with memories of the previous season's violent League match still fresh, this wretched Cup-tie must surely have caused them to lose some friends at a time when friends were needed.

This was the first season in which South Shields home games clashed with those of Sunderland instead of Newcastle. The season that South Shields were experiencing would probably not have tempted many people to visit Horsley Hill even without the close proximity of First Division football, but the lure of Roker Park was graphically illustrated by an incident on 28 January.

When the home match with Hull City was postponed shortly before kick off time the South Shields players themselves ran for the bus to take them to the Sunderland v Manchester City Cuptie. In keeping with their season they witnessed a home defeat.

It has already been observed that luck was never a luxury that South Shields possessed. Again and again in this season of heavy defeats, press reports refer to its absence. Even a self confessed barracker who wrote to the Shields Daily Gazette to defend his actions in the face of much criticism pointed out that Nottingham Forest won 4-3 at Horsley Hill by scoring with their only four shots of the game. Preston North End were *"flattered"* by their 7-2 victory at Deepdale in February.

Since before Christmas nobody had entertained the slightest doubt that the Third Division (North) was where South Shields would be next season. The sailor, the bulldog and the urchin named Kidder who inhabited the Football Gazette cartoon looked increasingly despondent as they greeted various Orientals, swans, biscuitmen, Robin Hood etc.

The first victory since Southampton came on 11 February against Swansea. It is rare for a player to score hat tricks in both League games against the same opposition (and in the case of a struggling club it must be unique) but Jack Oxberry repeated his three goals, this time to better effect in a 3-1 win.

To nobody's great surprise he was transferred a few days later to Blackpool, hardly a Bank of England Club. His departure left Harry Wilson as the sole survivor of the 1919-20 season. The question arose - were South Shields FC a viable business concern when their assets were being disposed of with so little resistance? The answer wasn't long in coming.

The last fifteen games brought four victories compared to three in the first twenty seven. Hull City were beaten 1-0 despite their manager Bill McCracken persisting with his old offside trap and Southampton succumbed to the double. After a 3-2 win at Port Vale on Good Friday hopes of a second double were scotched when Vale won at Horsley Hill on Easter Monday.

The home victory over Chelsea, which seemed more of a giant killing than ever, was mostly due to the brilliance of goalkeeper Shevlin. The last "big name" club to visit Horsley Hill was West Bromwich Albion who won 3-2 on 28 April. Only a miracle could save South Shields and one duly occurred to extend their Second Division life - but only by a few minutes. In the last match at Bristol City vivid lightning and torrents of rain engulfed Ashton Gate at half time so the players were kept in the dressing room a little bit longer.

(1928/29) Third Division Days:
Lots Of Goals, Lots Of Fun, But Not Much Money

So it was the dreaded Third Division (North) where acquain-tance would be renewed with three old North Eastern League opponents. The trio were Ash-ington (whose finances were in a worse state than those of South Shields), Hart-lepools United and - a rather different case - newly elected Carlisle United, buoyant and optimistic as they embarked on their new adventure.

Shevlin, Shields' goalkeeper, clears the ball in the opening match at Darlington (a 2-2 draw)

.R. Phizacklea app-ealed to the League against the size of the transfer fee asked for him and it was reduced though seemingly to nobody's benefit as he was not re-engaged for the new season. New-comers included W. Reilly from Kil-marnock, John Scott from Oldham Athletic, G.H. Neilson from Durham City who had just left the League and - notably - Robert Kennedy who had scored 53 goals in two seasons for Falkirk.

In May a meeting of shareholders had been told of a profit of £1,205 but this fooled nobody. A director acknowledged that without the transfer of players the club would have ceased to exist. There was no criticism of the manager, Mr Douglass, who was considered to have done a good job. Much needed improvements had been made to the pavilion and board room and it was hoped that the previous arrangement whereby home matches did not clash with those of Sunderland would be reverted to. Why South Shields ever agreed to play at home on the same day as Sunderland is a mystery as they lost far more potential customers to Roker than they did St James's Park, but it was a situation they had to endure for the remainder of their short career.

Players continued to be transferred during the summer with veteran Harry Wilson joining Jack Oxberry at Blackpool, Sam Henderson went to Chelsea and Conaty to Crystal Palace. J

The new season began with a short trip to Darlington where four goals were shared. There were four more goals in the first home match a week later, all of them scored by South Shields, against Southport in a game which the Sunday Sun described as *"an exceedingly pleasant introduction to Third Division football"*.

A *"brilliant"* victory at Rochdale raised hopes of a swift return to the Second Division but successive defeats at Nelson and at home to New Brighton showed that it would not be plain sailing. Wanderer noted that South Shields had been upset by New Brighton's "kick and rush" tactics and had yet to adapt to Third Division football. Another single goal defeat followed at Wrexham where the referee, Mr Woods of Sheffield, described the game as *"the finest Third Division game he had ever seen"*.

Then came a high scoring game against Chesterfield at Horsley Hill with Matthewson and Maycock both netting twice in a 6-3 victory and it was becoming apparent that, whatever skill or status was lacking at this level, entertainment value could be high. After a draw at Barrow and a home win over Doncaster, South Shields travelled a short distance down the Durham coast to meet Hartlepools United. The special train load of

Maycock scores the last goal in the 6-3 thrashing of Chesterfield.

supporters accompanying them must have thought their money well spent as South Shields romped home to a 5-0 victory which could have been higher. The North Mail noted that *"Many Second Division clubs are sighing for the type of class football they produced in every department of the team.... all the Shields goals were the result of brilliant passing bouts"*. Tempers became frayed at the end of this memorable game with Reilly and goalkeeper Shevlin being booked, but nothing could detract from a fine performance.

A week later Carlisle United paid their first visit to South Shields as a League club. They had made an inspired start to their inaugural season, had topped the division and had an even bigger win of 8-0 over Hartlepools to their credit. No fewer than 1,500 of their supporters enjoyed the strangely unsung delights of the Carlisle - Newcastle railway line to swell the crowd to 9,157. Let the Sunday Sun reporter take up the story. *"By playing football of a wonderfully high standard which completely upset the calculations of their opponents South Shields accomplished a great achievement against Carlisle United at Horsley Hill winning by five goals for the second week in succession.... the game was.... contested*

at a strenuous pace throughout and was crammed with thrills. Shields excelled themselves. There was splendid understanding in every department of the team, and the business-like way they set about their task was delightful to watch. Every man on the Shields team played well".

In retrospect it would seem that these opening few weeks in the Third Division must rank among the happiest in the League history of the club, while these successive 5-0 victories stand comparison with the successful Christmas and New Year week of 1925-26.

Whilst it was true that clubs with famous names were no longer visiting, some of the matches against the smaller fry were producing football of a surprisingly high order. All the more distressing therefore that the days of League football in the town were as good as numbered.

An early exit from the FA Cup occurred at Accrington where South Shields lost the first round tie 2-1 in torrential rain. This match was sandwiched between two visits to Cheshire for games with completely dissimilar results. A good 5-1 victory over Crewe Alexandra was followed a fortnight later by a 7-1 defeat by old Second Division rivals Stockport County. Up to this stage Stockport's home form had been a phenomenon. They had already scored seven goals against Lincoln City and Darlington, six against Accrington Stanley and Wrexham and four against Tranmere Rovers, Ashington and Rochdale with only Carlisle United returning home with a point.

Another heavy defeat befell South Shields at Lincoln by 5-0 and results over the next month were patchy. Free scoring Bradford City were held 1-1 at Horsley Hill then a 3-1 victory at Ashington on Christmas Day was followed by a disappointing goalless draw against the same opponents twenty-four hours later. Three successive defeats at the hands of Darlington (at home) and away to Accrington and Southport, the latter by 5-0, signalled that promotion hopes were extinct and that the early season sparkle had evaporated.

After such a dismal run it should have come as no surprise that the crowd for the home game against Tranmere Rovers was the lowest of the season thus far. Perhaps it was the fact that Newcastle and Sunderland were both far away receiving their FA Cup dismissals at Swindon and West Ham respectively that led to the first appearance in print of an idea that had been rumoured for some time. It was simply this: Attendances had sunk to a level at which the club's continued existence was not sustainable. The directors were not prepared to go on financing the club at Horsley Hill but, rather than allowing it to die, were planning to move to another venue away from the town.

At this stage the Brough Park Stadium at Byker, a district of East Newcastle, was being inspected. Greyhound racing had recently commenced at this site and it had previously been the home of Newcastle City, a North Eastern League club who had not continued after the Great War.

To say that the news caused some consternation locally would be correct but as the cause of the crisis was widespread lack of interest the matter should be seen in its true perspective. Indeed it was hardly the major local story as the Shields Daily Gazette was devoting more attention to a proposed bridge to link the town with North Shields, something which would affect far more local people than had ever attended a match at Horsley Hill. Despite the 4-1 win over Tranmere the attendance for the next home game against Rochdale - another good victory by 5-2 - was scarcely any higher. *"Can anyone wonder that such a drastic view has been contemplated?. Evidently League football is not wanted in South Shields"* was the paper's editorial comment.

A match against Wrexham on 2 February was chiefly notable in that South Shields full back Dunn was sent off for fouling Wrexham's Longmuir, a decision which caused the Horsley Hill faithful to *"give vent to strong resentment which continued for sometime afterwards"*. (It must be observed that the number of South Shields players ordered off in such a short League career seems abnormally high in an era when the measure was rarely resorted to). The pitch was described as being in a *"wretched state"*, something that was now unlikely to alter. When Hartlepools United drew 1-1 on 2 March less than £200 was taken at the gate, prompting the Sunday Sun reporter to wonder how South Shields kept going at all. At Brunton Park a week later Carlisle United gained their revenge for the earlier defeat by reversing the 5-0 scoreline.

If the proposal to start a second League venue in Newcastle seemed unrealistic then an idea that had been mooted earlier in the decade in South Yorkshire sounds downright crazy. On 16 March South Shields entertained old Second Division rivals who had changed their name since their last visit. Rotherham County had managed to absorb their uppity neighbours Rotherham Town. The latter had applied to join the Football League - as if a town that had struggled to support one League club could have ever managed with two!

Wiser heads had prevailed and it was Rotherham United who stepped out at Horsley Hill that afternoon. The lowest crowd of the season assembled which was a pity as those who were there saw South Shields score in the seventh, fifteenth, twenty-first, thirtieth and thirty-third minutes with a Rotherham consolation in the fortieth. South Shields took rather longer to get into their stride after the interval but then they scored in the sixty-second, seventy-sixth, seventy-ninth, eighty-third and eighty-eighth minutes before missing a penalty in the dying seconds.

At least Rotherham hadn't equalled their heaviest defeat of the season as Bradford City had beaten them 11-1 on the opening day, eight of their team having played in both those matches. So who said there was no fun in watching South Shields? Centre forward Ranson Maycock scored four of them, equalling the record set by George Lillycrop in 1920, there were two each by Jimmy Stevenson and George Scott and one apiece for Kennedy and Matthewson, despite the last named being ill with a chill for which he was ordered to bed immediately after the match.

Wanderer, whose wandering days were almost over, enjoyed himself immensely. He recorded that South Shields *played like a team inspired and I have no doubt that if the game had lasted a few minutes longer they would have surpassed all previous scoring records in English League football"*. He described the forwards as *"absolutely irresistible and they owed their remarkable success to the accuracy and forcefulness of their finishing efforts. They were quick to snap up practically every chance that came their way and completely broke down an opposition, which at one time threatened to be of a somewhat stubborn character. In every department it was a splendidly balanced team..... The South Shields intermediate men, though not so much in the limelight as their colleagues in front, are entitled to a big share of the credit for their splendid victory.*

"They not only established the mastery of the Rotherham forwards but also joined with the attack in the execution of impressive team work". And he had some good words for Rotherham too *".... not a team to be despised.... there were times when they came very near to bringing about a substantial reduction in the arrears".*

The 10-1 victory was followed by a 4-0 defeat at Wigan but three successive home games yielded maximum points against Accrington Stanley, Crewe Alexandra and Nelson. There was a little bit of crowd trouble when Stockport County completed the double at Horsley Hill and the midweek home game with Barrow postponed from earlier drew the lowest gate yet of 1,468.

Another small crowd saw Lincoln City defeated on 27 April. This may have been affected by a new counter attraction. The FA Cup Final was being broadcast on the radio. The nearest South Shields had ever got to the FA Cup Final was when they had played at Fulham on the Final Days of 1920 and 1923. Wembley seemed less remote that day because not only was old Horsley Hill favourite Jack Smith playing for Jack Tinn's Portsmouth team, who lost 2-0 to Bolton Wanderers, but there was much satisfaction locally that the game was being refereed by a South Shields man, Mr A. Josephs, a schoolteacher who had once played half back for South Shields reserves and had been secretary of the second team at Horsley Hill.

The highest crowd at Horsley Hill that season had been 9,157 against Carlisle but more than three times that number were at Valley Parade on 4 May to see record goalscorers Bradford City celebrate promotion by beating South Shields 3-

(1929/30) Farewell To Shields

The shareholders meeting in May was not an optimistic one. *"If we don't get better support than we received last season there won't be any club after next season"*, warned the chairman Mr Gray as he noted that the previous year's profit of £1,205 had been succeeded by a loss of £3,000. Manager Ernie Douglass was being honest though not very helpful when he observed that, *"there is no getting away from the fact that their is a tremendous difference in the class of football now on offer"*, and that if people preferred to watch First Division football a short distance away they could hardly be blamed.

Season ticket sales were encouraging however and the team themselves, playing in new colours of claret and blue, began well enough with a victory at Chesterfield on the opening day. After losing at Doncaster the fixture list threw up four consecutive home games. Three of these were won but the exception, a 5-1 defeat at the hands of Tranmere Rovers, was not to the liking of "Onside" who had replaced Wanderer as the Shields Daily Gazette reporter. He described how *"some of the Dismal Desmonds left the field on Saturday with faces all awry and talking as though the end of all things had come in South Shields football.... that South Shields, however, are nearing the parting of the ways is an obvious fact"*.

Some famous faces were appearing in the Horsley Hill press box. Colin Veitch the celebrated Newcastle United captain in the pre-war "Golden Era" had reported the match against Doncaster Rovers but was appalled by the low

SOUTH SHIELDS "GATES."

TRADE DEPRESSION NOT SOLE CAUSE OF POOR SUPPORT.

The South Shields directors' hint at transferring the activities of the club to another centre if greater support is not forthcoming at Horsley Hill met with no great response at the team's home game with Rochdale yesterday, when the attendance was about the same as at the Tranmere match the previous week.

One director declared to a "Sunday Sun" representative: "I was disgusted with this afternoon's gate. We are not getting sufficient money to pay wages, and we simply cannot carry on at this rate. We ought to have had at least double the gate we had to-day."

He added that before the club could be transferred to another centre the shareholders would have to be consulted, but declined to say anything further on the matter.

Asked as to whether he thought the meagre attendances were the result of the prolonged trade depression in the town, he replied, "Trade depression is undoubtedly very bad, but I do not consider that it accounts for the smallness of the attendance at our league matches.

Charabanc loads of people left the town yesterday for the Sunderland match at Roker Park.

Back in January 1929 there had been talks about a move.

attendance and thought that the directors *"were flogging a dead horse"*. A more frequent visitor was Stan Seymour whom South Shields had been interested in signing several years earlier but who had now completed his playing career at Newcastle and was reporting matches at South Shields and elsewhere for the Sunday Sun.

The season proceeded in rather lacklustre fashion with more victories than defeats and on 31 October a well attended public meeting appealed for better support. Fleeting cause for optimism followed when the next match against eventual champions Port Vale drew the biggest gate of the season, 5,984, who witnessed a goalless draw. *"It was something like old times"* said the Gazette reporter whilst an exiled "Noisy North Ender" wrote from Southampton to say that the three games he had seen at Horsley Hill that season were better than those he had seen at the Dell *"so come on you supporters and let the old cry of 'one, two three, what a beauty' ring out from the North Stand."*

A lucrative Cup run would have helped but first round visitors Wrexham had other ideas. Arriving an hour late because of railway troubles they made up for lost time by racing to a 3-0 half time lead and, changing ends without a break, ended their hosts' cup career with a 4-2 win in appalling weather. The Shields Daily Gazette noted curiously that *"having regard to the bad visibility from the press box the windows of which were practically opaque owing to vapour, it would not be too wise to apportion responsibility for the defeat too individually"*.

Stan Seymour saw enough to put much of the blame down to a poor display by goalkeeper Carr.

South Shields reserves were having an unsuccessful season in the North Eastern League but a 6-2 defeat by Spennymoor United had its compensations. Impressed by Spennymoor's centre forward Henry B Barkas who had scored four of them, South Shields signed him on. In an era more given to literary allusion than the present it was observed that *"Barkas was willing"* and he was certainly able for he ended the season as second highest scorer. Two of these goals came on his debut against Nelson when the small crowd was pleased to see the recently transferred Peter Shevlin playing in goal for the visitors and long-standing favourite Jimmy Metcalf in their half back line.

Christmas was not a happy one and New Year was worse. After losing 4-1 at Carlisle on 21 December South Shields found themselves without a goalkeeper. An amateur, T. E. Brown, was found with difficulty. His brief League career constituted of two games against Hartlepools whose achievement in taking maximum points in winning 2-1 at the Victoria Ground and 5-3 at Horsley Hill must have given them much satisfaction.

A brief respite occurred when Chesterfield were defeated 3-1 at Horsley Hill but New Years Day took South Shields to Darlington and an 8-3 defeat. Only Matthewson remained from the side that had lost 8-2 at the same ground on 23 April 1927, but this second heavy defeat by old North Eastern League rivals coming so soon after the pointless Christmas games would no doubt have provided food for thought for the "Dismal Desmonds" referred to earlier.

As the hungry twenties gave way to the troubled thirties there seems to have been general consensus that League football would be leaving South Shields. Little had been heard of schemes to relocate for sometime however and it still seemed likely that Newcastle would be the club's new location.

Suspicion was aroused with the election of a new director whose home was at Gosforth, a well to do area where there was a stadium. The reactions of Newcastle United and Sunderland were interesting. Both clubs had been friendly to South Shields throughout their League career - not least in the payment of transfer fees which had kept the club alive - but self interest was now beginning to assert itself. Sunderland let slip a broad hint that they would not be sorry if their near neighbours left the area. Newcastle United were said to be *"lukewarm"* to the proposal of a second League club appearing in the city and in mid-February they voiced their objections to the Football League who refused permission for the move.

A report that the South Shields board had inspected a site in the populous town of Gateshead was denied at first, but much credence was attached to this suggestion and on 22 March, Football League permission was granted and the club announced that they would be playing in that town the following season. A new Stadium was to be built and would be known as Redheugh (pronounced *Red-yoof*) Park. Gateshead Town Council had been very welcoming and work on turfing the ground and erecting stands was to commence immediately. South Shields Council on the other hand were issuing a Distress Warrant on the club for non-payment of rates at Horsley Hill.

The doomed club completed their fixtures but interest was low. Ten years earlier a supporter suggested in a letter to a newspaper that the club should provide entertainment such as a band as crowds were so large that it was necessary to arrive an hour before kick off. How times had changed. When old whipping boys Rotherham arrived on 1 February (South Shields won 5-0 this time) it was noted that *"the attendance was so small that when the ball went over the rails the players more often than not had to go and retrieve it themselves"*.

Stan Seymour's report of the match against New Brighton on 15 March is worth quoting at length.

After noting that spectators had shouted *"Come on Gateshead"*, Seymour observed that *"Never have I seen South Shields give such a woeful display.... I agreed with a prominent director of a first class club, who came all prepared to do business, who remarked "I will not trouble to take the forms out of my pocket". When I saw New Brighton's team I fully expected Shields to win because most of their visitors are long service players. Two of their prominent members are Jock MacDonald, the old Everton player, and Walter Wadsworth, who used to be with Liverpool. Many are the struggles and hefty ones I have had against these stalwarts, but they both have a good kick left in them yet.... [New Brighton goalkeeper] H. Ward had never played in League football before.... By his antics I quite believed it, and it was well for the visitors that he never got a difficult shot to stop all game".*

Maycock scores in the home match versus York City.

These pungent comments tell us much about the Third Division (North) and could serve as its epitaph. Overall skill was low but the Division served a dual purpose, firstly as a shop window for promising youngsters (though none were on display in this match) and secondly it extended the careers of men such as those whom Seymour described (politely) as *"long service players"*. In referring to their *"hefty struggles"* and their *"good kick"* Stan Seymour was thinking of a series of rough games between Newcastle and Liverpool in the twenties in one of which he had been seriously injured. Wadsworth had been one of three players sent off in one of those matches at Anfield in 1925. His only previous visit to Horsley Hill had been in the Liverpool defence *"merciless in its methods"* in the FA Cup-tie of 1920. Other reports were more complimentary to

New Brighton 'keeper Ward, here making his only League appearance, and New Brighton's blend of youth and experience triumphed over South Shields by 2-1.

Interest had now hit rock bottom but there were still a few highlights. Ranson Maycock scored a hat trick against Southport - *"Shields Sparkle"* read a Sunday Sun headline - and Thomas Charlton scored another one against Carlisle United. By far the largest crowd for the latter stages of that strange season - 4,777 - saw Darlington draw 3-3 on Good Friday. Perhaps this merely continued the tradition of higher attendances on public holidays or perhaps it suggested that matches of some local significance were still of more interest than games against unknown visitors from far away.

The directors had lamented that North Eastern League matches against Sunderland reserves attracted as many people to the ground as did some League matches. In the cold light of reason it had all been a great mistake. South Shields should have remained in the North Eastern League. But then they would never have been 'The Team That Beat Leeds United.' There had been ups as well as downs, thick as well as thin. Recall those glowing reports of the 7-1 win over Hull City in 1920 and the League victory over Derby County in 1925, the victories at Preston and Middlesbrough over the 1925-26 holiday period, stirring Cup-ties with large attendances, more recently the consecutive 5-0 triumphs over Hartlepools and Carlisle Uniteds, the player capped for England and transferred for the record fee (though much good it did them). Famous visitors, great games. Of all defunct Football League clubs none crammed as much into a short and colourful career as did South Shields.

The last goal ever at Horsley Hill, in the Accrington Stanley match.

If the object of a football club is to provide entertainment and interest then South Shields succeeded in supplying both to poor people in hungry times. Luck was never on their side and if there had ever been any intention of rivalling their giant neighbours on the Tyne and Wear then surely it was an unrealistic one.

Little consolation to be sure but South Shields never hit rock bottom in the average attendance figures League. (Another Tyneside club did so in later years but we mustn't anticipate). Even the paltry 3,300 average in Horsley Hill's last season as a League venue was appreciably higher than that at Southern Section Merthyr Town who were also leaving the League and whose players included Richard Parker who had recently left South Shields.

Recall how ambitious South Shields had paid a large fee for his namesake not long ago and how he had gone on to score very few goals for South Shields and very many for other clubs. There were still several former Shieldsmen in the League and one of the best of them would be taking a last bow at Horsley Hill.

After the two last away games were won there came the fine victory over Carlisle then "Tricky" Hawes (*"He still carries the hanky about with him"*) played for Accrington Stanley in the last South Shields match at Horsley Hill - a 2-2 draw before 1,752 spectators.

When August came around nine of that last South Shields team played together against Doncaster Rovers elsewhere. But that's another story.

THE PROMISED LAND.

J. DOXFORD-30

Here's wishing them the very best of luck !

GOOD AND BAD

Now that the Hill has "gone to the dogs," many of the habitues recall outstanding games played there. The following three games stand out most vividly. Firstly, the Players Union XI versus the North-East, the latter eleven being chosen from the "big four." Rarely must this game have been eclipsed for football as it should be played.

Included in the North-East side, were, such players as the one and only, Charlie Buchan, George Elliot, George Kienley side and Wilf Low. This game was such a success that the Hill was chosen for another representative match, but on this occasion several of the players failed to appear. This match was a farce and the spectators did not forget to let the players know it. The result was that a resolution was passed that never again would one of these "representative" games would be allowed at the Hill.

What must rank as one of the hardest fought games was that between South Shields and Sunderland reserve teams in the final of the Sunderland Shipowners' Cup.

It was only after extra time that the Shields team won, as a result of a penalty taken by Jack Oxberry, who burst the net with a terrific drive.—T. SALES, 15 Regent Street, South Shields.

SOUTH SHIELDS SUPPORTERS REMINISCE

(A selection of readers letters, from the Football Gazette' of 1932

AT HORSLEY HILL

South Shields having received their Second Division baptism the Saturday before, at Fulham, a great crowd turned up at "the Hill" and, after running Fulham to a 1-0 defeat Shields were confident of taking two points.

Fulham commenced in fine style but were met with a stout defence and, after many thrilling duels in both goals half-time came with no score.

After the interval the visitors set the pace and played a keen aggressive game with direct methods, but the Shields defence was as firm as a rock.

After some accurate passing by the Shields right wing, J. J. Ball, the centre forward scored for Shields. After this Fulham were often dangerous and Hoffman had many shots to deal with, but, in a sharp exchange, Billy Frith, the Shields half-back, scored with a terrific drive amid tremendous cheering and, with the Shields defence still holding, the whistle went for the final, and Shields had won 2-0.—TOM PRIOR, 127 Adelaide Street, South Shields.

SHIELDS' FIRST GOAL

It was Monday evening and Shields were making their first appearance at home in the Football League. Birmingham provided the opposition. At half time there was no score, darkness set in and you couldn't see the opposite goalmouth.

The local keeper was at the sea-end. His half and full-backs were joining in the siege on the Birmingham goal. Two minutes to go. Something had happened at the dark end. There was a great shout and out of the gloom came a struggling mass of "red and green" shirts, half dragging something with them. It was Archie Roe.

In the desperate onslaught he had scrambled the ball through and scored Shields first goal in the Second Division. The game restarted. There were shouts of Howway Shields, Keep thim oot. Birmingham came up with a rush; hearts beat faster, the whistle went. Time!—THOMAS HESLOP, 81 Frederick Street, South Shields.

QUEER MATCH

It happened at "the Hill", South Shields v. Clapton Orient. A tame opening and rough play with Orient's centre forward ordered off. Five minutes later Shields' left back was ordered off. Then came two fine goals by Oxberry, for Shields, and an unorthodox display at left back by Harry Wilson.

In the second half Shields scored again through Keenlyside, while Orient lost Nicholson injured.—D. DOCKWRAY, 64 Broughton Road, South Shields.

DO YOU REMEMBER?

I shall never forget the game between South Shields Reserves and Newcastle Reserves, at Horsley Hill, a few years ago.

Little did yo dream we were going we should see Shields win 9—0. Nevertheless that happened. Nor was it one-sided.

Newcastle had their usual good side and play was good, considering there was snow on the ground. Newcastle could do anything that day but get the ball into the net and Shields could not miss the goal.

I remember Matthewson coming out at half-time with a piece of lemon. He got the ball from the kick-off and lifted it into the air towards the Newcastle goal. It bounced and landed in the net. He could not eat his lemon for laughing, and threw it in the cinder track. All eyes were on the poor goal-keeper, who was making his first appearance for Newcastle Reserves that day. If I am not mistaken that goal-keeper afterwards made good.—J. DEFTY, 103 Lytton Street, South Shields.

ON THE MAP

I have in my possession a Sunderland football programme dated Saturday, January 30th, 1915. On that day Sunderland played South Shields in a Durham County cup-tie. Sunderland, having no first division match, put out a strong team against Shields and, although they won after a hard and exciting game there was not much to spare.

A great crowd of followers from Shields and district brought the gate to 14,000. Shields was on the map in those days. The teams were as follows:

Sunderland.—Scott; Gladwin, Ness; Cuggy, Hopkins, Coverdale; Mordue, Buchan; Moore, Phillip, Martin.

South Shields.—Naisby; Johnson, Stott; Low, Robinson, Hall; Bridgett, Hall, Thornley, Whittingham, Keenlyside. JOHN G. FOSTER, 17 Rosa Street, South Shields.

GOALKEEPER'S DAY OFF

When South Shields, Second Division, Reserves were playing Chester-le-Street at Horsley Hill in a North-Eastern League match, they had a chap called Brown, giving him a try out.

The outside left of Chester-le-Street centred the ball which would have gone out of play by the off side post (Chester-le-St. were kicking towards the bob-end goal) had not Brown stepped sideways to catch the ball, instead of letting it go out.

Anyway the ball hit him and it went in "a goal".

Not long afterwards there was another poor shot. The ball was slowly rolling out of play by the same post with nobody handy, except the home goalkeeper. He stepped off the playing pitch, picked up the ball, and threw it down for the left back to place for a goal kick. The referee hadn't blown his whistle.

Like a flash, Harvey, the Chester-le-Street centre forward, rushed in and scored—"two up".

The goalkeeper was out of play but his hands were not, neither was the ball. The spectators had a good laugh.

This happened in the first half, and it was all Shields after that, but no score. So Chester-le-Street took the points away, winning 2-0.

It was hard luck for Brown. One never knows how good he may have been, I don't think he played for Shields again.— R. CUMMINGS, 17 Roman Road, South Shields.

SHIELDS " MYSTERY " MAN

I remember the match at the Hill, South Shields v. Bradford Park Avenue, one New Year.

We were waiting for the kick-off, when the board came round showing one change. It was a new centre-forward. We all wondered who he was. We soon found out, for he scored four goals.

He was on trial from Hull City. It was J. Smith, born in South Shields.— A. E. BULMER, 158 Stanhope Road, South Shields.

URGED THEM ON

An old Shields supporter, I often visualise the times I spent at Horsley Hill.

I used to frequent, together with a group of others, the wooden terraced part of the " bob end," even when the concession in the East stand admission charge was made. There were about ten of us in this group, and some, being in casual employment, had to scrape a little for their admission charge, but still enjoyed their Saturday treat. Often, when Shields were hard pressed, we would be heard giving vocal support, together with the sound of the bell that one enthusiast used to ring from the North Stand.

Occasionally I meet some of the old supporters at Gateshead and talk over old times at the Hill, memories of which I shall always treasure.—E. CHAPMAN, 17 Rutland Street, Tyne Dock.

WELL TRAINED

When South Shields was on the football map most of their successes were due to the way they were trained, so let me pay tribute to the way George Lilycrop trained his players. All the players were tried out each morning, in some course or other, under Lilycrop's watchful eye. His advice to the players was also very useful. I regret that I can't see them train now.—T. DINSDALE, 9 Hampden Street, South Shields.

Miscellany

Police Court Jottings

Whilst the South Shields players were a tough bunch on the field they seem to have led unblemished lives off it. Only one misdemeanour has been found and that was long before the playing days of the person concerned. Whilst researching the South Shields Northern Rugby Union club, a police court item of 1903 was noticed which concerned a named 12 year-old boy being fined. Throwing stones is a dangerous activity so perhaps it is a mercy that Ernie Simms was always a much better shot when he was away from the North East than he ever was at South Shields.

The poor performance of Port Vale goalkeeper Smith in conceding six goals at Horsley Hill on 23 October 1920 was partially due to the fact that he was under arrest and had to be bailed out of custody to play in the match. The charge was one of assault involving a female hotel employee, and a detective was watching the him from the stand. It should be stressed that, when the case came up at Durham Assizes, Smith was acquitted.

On the evening of 17 March 1924 an explosion was heard at Horsley Hill and it was later found that an attempt had been made to blow open the club safe. This attempt to rob South Shields F.C. of their great riches was futile as the takings of that afternoon's match against Crystal Palace were already at the bank.

To conclude this review of misdemeanours on a light note, reference should be made to a strange case which was heard at South Shields Magistrates Court on 11 April 1925, arising out of incidents at the home game against Southampton on 21 March. The match referee heard a critical remark made about him in which bad language was alleged to have been used. The official left the pitch and performed a citizen's arrest of a spectator who was ejected from the ground and charged with conduct likely to cause a breach of the peace. The defendant, who came from North Shields (Coronation Street no less), agreed that he had made the remark but had never sworn in his life and was a former referee himself. Nearby spectators had not heard any bad language used and an uncomprehending Magistrate dismissed the case after musing over the practical difficulties of prosecuting everybody who swore at football matches. The referee, Mr. Harper of Stourbridge, cannot have borne a grudge against the North-East as he is chiefly remembered for having allowed a disputed goal which Newcastle scored against Arsenal in the 1932 Cup Final!

The FA Cup - Pre-Football League

At first South Shields had to play in the earliest qualifying rounds of the FA Cup against some very minor opponents. Their eliminators in the first few seasons were Workington, Willington Athletic, North Shields Athletic (after three money-spinning games in the 1910-11 season) and Newcastle City. In the 1912-13 season they beat a Second Division club, Lincoln City, 1-0 in the fifth qualifying round. They were then drawn at home to Gainsborough Trinity whose own Football League career had recently ended. This match was abandoned at half time because of a gale (South Shields had been leading 1-0). When it was replayed a week later, full back English McConnell opted to play for South Shields despite being selected to play for Ireland against Wales; Gainsborough won 1-0.

In the 1913-14 season, after winning 1-0 at Hartlepools, South Shields won 2-0 at home to Luton Town of the Southern League in a replay. Luton fielded a former and two future South Shields players (Simms and Mitchell). There seems to have been some sort of friendship between these two clubs as several men played for both. In the next round South Shields travelled to Burnley of the First Division, losing 3-1 to the eventual Cup winners. The following season South Shields lost 2-1 at home to Fulham in the first round.

Travelling Fans

It does not seem to have been uncommon, even in 1914, for large numbers of supporters to travel 100 miles and more to matches, especially Cup-ties. During the Twenties, South Shields supporters would travel as far as Bradford and Sheffield whilst Hull City brought several hundred of theirs to Horsley Hill on at least one occasion.

The report (right) - relating to the 1913-14 season match - makes strange reading with these travellers being shown round the inner workings of Turf Moor, and bringing home clogs and shawls as cultural mementoes of a visit to Lancashire. For once we may sigh with envy for the days *"when lads knew how to behave."* On the other hand how many of this trainload would be buried in France and Belgium when South Shields played their first Football League match five years later?

The 'Six-and-a tanner' title, amounts to six shillings and sixpence - 32p. *"Poor Newcastle"* refers to Sheffield United's 5-0 Cup-tie victory at St. James's Park that day.

THE BURNLEY TRIP.

Jerky Jottings by a Six-and-a-Tanner Tripper.

It was raining at 7 o'clock last Saturday morning, but it gladdened our hearts to see nearly 400 enthusiastic supporters, including a score of ladies, at the station to take the journey to Burnley. The "Laddie's" colours were in evidence. We observed the little mascot with his football and envied the man in the clicking and [illegible]. The train was a long one, with four saloons attached.

We leave with bugle calls, and pick up some supporters on the way up to Newcastle. We settle down to the journey. Of course, the main topic is the match. Are the players fit? What will be the team? The prevailing opinion is that Burnley will get a fright!

Darlington is reached. Shades of the Durham Senior Cup! Revenge in a fortnight! Songs and games keep us alive until we reach Burnley after 1 o'clock. It's now fair. We see the team and officials arrive at Turf Moor. Every man looks fit.

What's the team? Not picked until they see the ground. Forty and Joe Smith are playing. We admire the beautiful offices, [illegible]-rooms, baths, billiard-room and [illegible] under the [illegible] stand. We find it is the only stand on the field but that they are going to build a double-decker shortly on the opposite side.

The field is covered with mud. That should suit our lads. They will think they are near the Trow Rocks. The rival mascots cause great laughter. Little [illegible] cannot pick up all the coppers the Lancashire folk are throwing to him. The ambulance men help him.

They are off! Play up the 'Laddie! You have heard all about the match. We are pleased to hear one of the Burnley officials say that South Shields could beat all the teams in the Second Division and half the teams in the First. He meant it, too.

We get into an hotel for tea, and the room is full of Lancashire folk talking about the match. We are not known, they were agreeably surprised at the clean high-class football played by South Shields. Knew all about the club's record in the North-Eastern League, and how many goals Thornley and Brideson had scored. One even knew that South Shields was at the mouth of the Tyne and had a bigger population than Burnley. A town is known by the football club it keeps!

They would not have been surprised to see a draw. Shields were worth it. They should certainly be playing in better class. Couldn't Burnley do with Kennyside? Bridgett still a star. Full-backs excellent. Centre-half a marvel. If inside forwards had taken their chances different story would have been told. Nothing but good opinions about our team.

We get to Manchester, where the fire brigade showed us how to turn out. We are beaten there! The orchestra at the Hippodrome's on strike. Could we get a start? We can muster a bugle and four [illegible]. No, we won't blackleg! We see the show. The top of the bill, "Say When!" was a bit of all right.

Tommy thought he knew the road to the station but he led us astray, and we had to consult a man in blue. We left Manchester at 11.50, and changed at Todmorden.

About one o'clock on the Sunday morning and the station is in semi-darkness. We are hustled from one platform to another by the solitary porter, and find our carriages, but they are in darkness, and our seats are occupied. We manage to get a light and help the porter to attach our carriages to the right engine.

At last we leave Todmorden. One chap has passed his station and will persist in getting out of the moving train. Heaven save him from injury! We hear faintly "It's a long, long way from Burnley," and "I didn't want to do it." We hear the best joke. Our friend in the corner travelled in the dark train from Burnley and dozed off to sleep. He awoke near Todmorden and said, "As think we were through this bleedin' tunnel" (The stations are only nine miles apart). Our friend has followed the "Laddie" for 17 years, and has a brilliant idea about the straight cross line of the team.

It's 3 a.m. Thanks Arthur for the [illegible] and you, too, Teddy, for the butter drops! They are very acceptable. One by one we doze off. Teddy cuddles into Jacob. Newcastle is reached. Poor Newcastle! At 5.45, we are at Shields. Our friend with the brilliant idea cannot find his cap. He ties heads in his handkerchief and says, "What odds. The wife'll be in bed. As divent care so long as as got the clogs and shawls as bowt for the bairns."

There they are again! Arthur, Sammy, Irvine (with a plaster over his eye), Forty, George, Ellis, Ben, Joe, and Charlie. All still looking in the pink. Never mind, lads. You did your best. Nobody will grumble. We are tired. Down-hearted? No! No! We will go further next year if we can raise the tin.—"O.T."

Players' Profiles

The following entries contain varying amounts of information concerning the 121 men who played for South Shields in the Football League. They include men who played in Cup Finals and at International level before and after their South Shields days (in the case of one International - during them), men whose football careers spanned several years with many clubs and others with only one appearance to their name. There are no 'household' names, and some are so obscure that South Shields supporters of the day would not know them. Some sort of prize ought to go to Chape - his only appearance was at Bradford City in midweek; no North Eastern newspaper printed the line-ups and when reference was made to the *Bradford Telegraph and Argus* it was found that his name had been obliterated by a blemish in the print! In the initial 1919-20 season players seemed to appear as if from nowhere, play a couple of games, and then vanish.

One player was born in Australia, two in Ireland, one each in Cheshire, Derbyshire, Hampshire, Norfolk and Warwickshire, four in Lancashire, a little bunch in Yorkshire (Sheffield crops up a lot), and there were several Scots, but the overwhelming majority were natives of North Eastern England; nearby Sunderland and East Durham supplied many. *"Yes, he's a mak'em and tak'em and proud of it"* said a 1920 profile of Johnny Oxberry.

When their playing days were over some returned to the mines whilst others spent the rest of their working lives in the employment of football clubs. One man was a prominent county cricketer (a popular sport with many of them), and another became a cattle rancher in Argentina. A few died young, others lived well into their nineties. Very few received an obituary notice. The deaths of managers Jack Tinn in 1971 and Ernie Douglass in 1963 went unnoticed by the local press.

It was not uncommon for players to understate their age; Maitland and Thirlaway were found to be two years older than they had stated. Laurie Crown seems to have deceived a lot of people with his birthdate of 29 February 1898 (it wasn't a leap year!). Conversely William Hampson was found to be two years younger than previously thought.

FRANK ATKINSON   1926-27
A Northumbrian born full-back who played two games in March 1926. His third (and unsurprisingly last) game was in a 7-2 defeat at Nottingham Forest in September 1927. Later that season a newspaper reported that he had gone to Dundee FC on a free transfer but he never played a first team game there.

SIMPSON BAINBRIDGE   1920-21
A winger whose career began at Aberdare where he represented England Schoolboys against Wales in 1908 and ended at Aberdeen for whom he played 22 games in the 1921-22 season. Most of his career was spent with Leeds City before and (briefly) after the War. When the City players were put up for auction he became a Preston North End player but failed to win a regular First Division place and arrived at South Shields the following summer. Born in Silksworth on 3 April 1895 he died in Sunderland on 12 November 1988.

HENRY BROWN BARKAS   1929-30
Centre-forward Henry Barkas was born into a footballing family in Wardley, Gateshead, on 21 January 1906. After scoring four goals for Spennymoor United against South Shields Reserves he signed for the club and became a high scorer in the last League season at Horsley Hill. In December 1930 he was transferred from Gateshead to Liverpool but only made five First Division appearances without scoring. Henry Barkas died in 1974 at South Shields.

JOHN JAMES BELL   1919
Bell who was born in South Shields on 2 March 1891 assisted his home town club at the start of their League career. A man of many clubs he also played for Reading, Plymouth Argyle, Nottingham Forest, Merthyr Town, Grimsby Town, Albion Rovers, Newport County, Hartlepools United and Watford.

ROBERT COLTMAN BOLAM   1923
Robert Bolam was born in Birtley, Co.Durham, in 1896. Before joining South Shields he had played for Sheffield United in the First Division and Darlington in the Third Division (North). The autumn of 1923, when Bolam made his 18 appearances for South Shields, was a good time to be there as the club led the table for much of that time. He transferred to Queens Park Rangers but only made two more appearances before leaving the game He died in Gateshead on 20 June 1964.

JOSEPH HAYES BRAYSON   1919
A youth from Newburn who had interested Aston Villa, Joseph Brayson made two appearances on the right-wing for South Shields at Stockport and Wolverhampton over the Christmas period of 1919. He later played for Ashington. He was born on 12 December 1901 and died in Newcastle on 13 May 1970.

BROWN R.   1928
An otherwise unknown half-back who played for South Shields at Grimsby on 24 March 1928.

THOMAS E. BROWN   1929
A goalkeeping crisis arose over the Christmas holidays in 1929 and an amateur, Thomas E. Brown, was obtained from an RAF base at Wittering Wansford, Northamptonshire. Tom Brown's goaldays were not a success as Hartlepools United scored 7 against him over two matches.

THOMAS H. BROWN   1923-24
A Glaswegian winger born in 1896. After failing to make a League appearance for Cardiff City he spent a season with each of Bristol City, South Shields and Luton Town. The only League goal he ever scored was in the match against Bristol City, which the *Sunday Sun* reporter enjoyed so much.

WILLIAM CLARENCE BROWNING   1919
Described as "a Whitburn youth" when he made his only appearance at home to Clapton Orient during a goalkeeping crisis on 4 October 1919, Browning was born in that prolific footballer producing village in June 1893 and died there on 29 April 1950.

RALPH BURKINSHAW   1919
The two appearance that centre-forward Burkinshaw made against Fulham in the first and third South Shields games were the prelude to a thirteen year career, comprising more than 300 games for Bury, Bradford City and Wrexham. He had previously been with Sheffield Wednesday with whom his two brothers played. Born in Kilnhurst near Rotherham on 26 March 1898, he died in that area in 1951.

ANTHONY GRAY CARR   1929-30
The last regular South Shields goalkeeper, Carr missed only 2 games in season 1929-30. After making 80 appearances for Newport County between 1922 and 1924, Sheffield Wednesday paid £1,200 for him and never played him. He arrived at Horsley Hill from Preston North End. Leaving the game in 1930 he reappeared briefly with New Brighton in 1934-35. Carr was born in Old Hartley, Northumberland on 18 May 1901 and died there on 4 February 1968.

WALTER CASSON   1921-22

Walter Casson arrived from Blyth Spartans in the summer of 1921 and promptly scored in his first two matches. That concluded his scoring record, however, and he was transferred to Grimsby Town the following February, later playing for Exeter City. He died in Northumberland on 8 November 1965 aged 70.

JOHN CLEMENT CARRUTHERS   1921

After RAF service as a pilot, John Carruthers made 8 Football League appearances spread between three clubs. Joining South Shields from Preston Colliery (North Shields) he scored on his debut at home to Fulham. His other games were for Bradford City (4) and Blackpool (2). Born in North Shields in 1900 he died in Norton-on-Tees on 19 October 1959.

GEORGE CHAPE   1924

An obscure South Shields player. George Chape's only League appearance was at left-half away to Bradford City in April 1924. The following season he made four appearances for Hartlepools United He died in Sunderland on 8 March 1968 aged 66.

THOMAS CHARLTON   1929-30

A Jarrow youth, he made his debut in the last game of 1929. He put in some good performances just before the move to Gateshead with the highlight definitely being his hat-trick against Carlisle United in the penultimate Horsley Hill match.

WILLIAM GEORGE CHARLTON   1919-22

An unattractive feature of the Horsley Hill crowd was their tendency to barrack players and young William Charlton seems to have had a raw deal despite his useful scoring record. He later played 8 games for West Ham United, none during a brief stay at Cardiff, then got back into his stride with many goals for Newport County and Tranmere Rovers. (He scored for Tranmere in both games against South Shields in 1929-30). He then topped the North Eastern League scoring table in each of three seasons for Workington. He was no mean cricketer either, playing as a professional for a local side after the war, and once took four wickets for a single run in a Durham Senior League match in 1940. He was a coal merchant and a church warden.

Born in Sunderland on 11 October 1900, he died there on 20 June 1981. A much older brother, Edward, played for Fulham for many years.

THOMAS PHILIP CONATY   1927-28

Thomas Conaty made 2 appearances in the half-back line during the relegation season - away at Stoke and Notts County. Transferred to Crystal Palace the next season, he made 3 appearances for the Londoners and he later played for Barrow. A North Shields man, Conaty died locally on 21 January 1964 at the age of 57.

COLIN COOK   1928-29

Colin Cook's winning goal in his debut against Hull City - a low key Wednesday afternoon fixture in March 1928 - was far too late in the season to affect South Shields' chances of escaping relegation. He left the club in 1929 for a varied career in and out of the League. His record at Chesterfield, where he scored 37 goals in 50 appearances, eclipsed his handful of games for Bradford City, Luton and Northampton. Interspersed with these League clubs he saw service with North Shields, Crook Town and (finally) Horden. Born in North Shields on 9 January 1909 he died there on 15 September 1976.

THOMAS CREIGHTON   **1929**

A full-back who had played as a Junior International for Scotland vs Ireland in 1926-27. He signed from Scottish junior club Bo'ness but only played for South Shields once - in a 5-0 defeat at Carlisle.

WARNEFORD (Warney) CRESSWELL   **1919-22**

Warney Cresswell was a full back of such class that South Shields did well to hold on to him for as long as they did. Sunderland's gold took him to Roker where he missed very few games in the five years before he transferred to Everton in 1927. He made 306 appearances for Everton, gaining a Cup Winner's medal in 1933 and he played for England seven times. In later years he was manager of Port Vale then Northampton Town. He was born in South Shields on 5 November 1894 and died on 20 October 1973.

LAWRENCE CROWN   **1923-26**   *Warney Cresswell*

Born in Sunderland, Laurie Crown was a dependable full-back whose three goals were all from the penalty spot. Newcastle United paid £2,750 for him in 1926 but sold him to Bury a year later at a considerable loss after he had made only two appearances. He went on to give good service to Bury and Coventry City. Laurie Crown died in Newcastle on 6 July 1984.

ANDREW DAVIDSON   **1920**

Dr Davidson was an amateur who played regularly for South Shields Reserves. He came close to scoring on his only League appearance when he was centre-half in a poor game at home to Wolves on New Years Day of 1920.

JAMES DAVIES   **1927-30**

Born in Northwich, Cheshire, on 20 November 1901. This player signed for South Shields in July 1927 after a year with Charlton Athletic. A half-back he played in many games which South Shields lost heavily in 1927-28 and was an ever present the following season. He moved to Gateshead with the club and after two years there he transferred to Chesterfield.

CHARLES F. DEVAN   **1924-25**

A Scottish forward born in Girvan, Ayrshire and signed from Morton in the summer of 1924. South Shields looked destined for relegation and Devan only finished on the winning side once in twelve outings. He then transferred to Grimsby Town and later to Fulham. Typically, he scored a dozen goals for his later clubs but none for South Shields. Two of the dozen (one for each team) were scored *against* South Shields. Devan's last League match was at Horsley Hill on 8 October 1927 when, despite his goal for Fulham, South Shields won 2-1. Perhaps he thought that if *that* South Shields team could beat his present side it was time to call it a day!

FRANK DOCHERTY   **1922**

A Scottish Junior International from Bellshill. His performance in the match at Crystal Palace won him high praise but it proved to be his only League appearance for South Shields.

ROBERT STEPHENSON DONALD   **1921**

Born in Selby, Yorkshire in 1899. Donald played 10 games on the wing for South Shields in early 1921 being released once to play for Durham University.

The following season he played in Hartlepools United's first ever Football League match and in 1925, as a Bishop Auckland player, he won an Amateur International Cap against Wales. He died in Saudi Arabia on 28 December 1951.

HENRY DREYER   1919-21
A dependable half-back Henry Dreyer had played for South Shields in the North Eastern League in 1914-15. After assisting the club in their first two League seasons Dreyer transferred to Crystal Palace and later played for Southend United. He was born in Sunderland on 9 March 1892 and died there on 17 July 1953.

GEORGE APPLEBY DUNN   1927-29
Born in North Shields in 1902, George Dunn was a full-back whose five Second Division games all ended

Robert Faulkner

in defeat. He was often on the winning side in the lower divisions but on the wrong side of the referee in the home match against Wrexham on 2 February 1929. He was sent off for kicking an opponent (which he denied) and was suspended for a month.

ROBERT FAULKNER   1922-23
A Scotsman from Paisley, Faulkner had played nine First Division games for Blackburn Rovers and 50 Third Division (South) games for Queens Park Rangers. A winger with a noticeably unspectacular scoring rate (1 goal in 68 matches for his three clubs), the highlight of his career was probably South Shields' FA Cup victory over his old club Blackburn at Ewood Park.

He had more success "across the herring pond" (the expression used in a 1920's newspaper) when he was capped for Canada three times against the United States in 1925 and 1926 and played for professional clubs in Toronto, Philadelphia and Providence, Rhode Island.

FLYNN   1919
A man who played on the right-wing and scored on his only appearance at home to Nottingham Forest on 15 November 1919. A newspaper described him as a South Shields man who had formerly been with Barnsley but no further reference can be found.

ROBERT WILLIAM FRITH   1919-20
A former Luton Town player (nothing unusual at South Shields) and described as *"probably the heaviest player"*. Billy Frith arrived in 1919. He played in the first League match and scored *"a lovely goal"* from 30 yards out a week later (also against Fulham) but when Rotherham County arrived late in the season he was already with the visitors. A native of Derbyshire (born 1892) he died in Sheffield on New Years Day 1939. His son William played in the League and managed Port Vale and Coventry City.

JAMES GASCOIGNE   1924-25
Described as *"a sturdy young centre-half from Ferryhill"* (Co. Durham) his three appearances were all at home and resulted in two victories and one drawn game.

THOMAS D. GIBSON   1927
A young Glaswegian centre-forward who arrived from Manchester City in 1927 with the promising record of having played twice and scored twice. At South Shields, however, he failed to score in four appearances. All four games were lost, two of them heavily.

ANDREW D. GRAY 1921-23
Although Gray joined South Shields from Leadgate Park he had previously made two First Division appearances for Newcastle United. A speedy winger (as one would expect with him being an athletics champion) his form was consistently good. He was definitely an asset to the club despite his peculiar behaviour (detailed elsewhere) which sometimes caused credit to be given to others. He retired at the end of the 1922-23 season. Gray's father was the chairman of South Shields FC later in the twenties.

EDWARD E. GREENWELL 1921-25
A forward whose performances for the Easington Colliery team had interested Tottenham Hotspur. Greenwell however, spent his whole career with South Shields. He maintained a fair scoring rate during the 'goal famine' years. Born in Wardley, Gateshead in 1901 he died at Easington Colliery on 29 August 1965.

Edward Greenwell

ALAN GRENYER 1924-29
Alan Grenyer had left North Shields Athletic in 1910 and spent 14 years with Everton. A right half-back he had won a Championship medal in the 1914/15 season and a 'Victory' International cap against Wales. He only played once in the first two years after joining South Shields in 1924, but became a regular player in the struggling seasons of 1926-28. Thereafter he became assistant trainer and in 1929 he crossed the Tyne to assist his native North Shields club as a trainer. He remained in that occupation until his death in April 1953. His son, also Alan, played for the later South Shields club.

GEORGE WOOD GUYAN 1924-26
George Guyan was born in Aberdeen on 5 April 1901 and joined South Shields from Dundee, making his debut in January 1924. In three years at Horsley Hill his appearances were sporadic but his scoring rate was impressive and Hull City paid a large fee for him in December 1926. After a similar spell at Hull he wandered off to many far flung clubs - Connahs Quay (where he won a Welsh cup medal), Exeter City, Swindon Town, Rochdale and Bath City.

WALKER HAMPSON 1919-21
A Burnley half-back before the War, Hampson was living in the North East and joined South Shields from Scotswood shortly after the beginning of the 1919-20 season. After two years of assisting South Shields, Hampson went South to play for the newly elected Charlton Athletic club and played in their first match. He later played for Hartlepools United and Chesterfield. Born in Radcliffe, Lancashire on 24 July 1889 he died in Bury on 28 June 1959.

WILLIAM HAMPSON 1927-28
in what looks like an act of desperation South Shields signed a 43 year old full-back who played 25 games in 1927-28. Bill Hampson had seen better days with Bury, Norwich City and (especially) Newcastle United with whom he had gained a cup winners medal in 1924. He was later manager of Carlisle and Leeds Uniteds. Walker Hampson's brother, he was born in Radcliffe on 26 August 1884 and died in Congleton on 23 February 1966.

JOHN JAMES HARDY 1921-24, 1927-28
Born in Sunderland on 10 February 1899, and signed from junior football there, centre-half Hardy rarely missed a match between 1921 and 1924. The decline of the club must have been very apparent when he returned in 1927 after playing for Derby, Grimsby and Oldham. He was still involved with the game until shortly before his early death from pneumonia in January 1932.

WILLIAM JAMES HARRIS   1924

Born in Cramlington, Northumberland, on 25 April 1900, William Harris' two games for South Shields were both at home and both were lost, at the beginning of the 1924-25 season. He had failed to make a first team appearance during spells with Coventry and Huddersfield but gained experience with Ashington and Wrexham. He was more successful as a professional sprinter winning handsome cash prizes at least twice. One of these victories was in the Morpeth Sprint and he died in that Northumbrian town on 5 April 1969.

ARTHUR HAWES   1920-21

A Norfolk man 'Tricky' Hawes arrived at South Shields from Norwich city in 1920. His 17 goals in 38 games led to his transfer to Sunderland and five years regular First Division appearances. After 1927 his football was played in the Third Division (North) with Champions Bradford (Park Avenue), run of the mill Accrington Stanley, and then two of the worst teams in history - Nelson of 1930-31 and Rochdale of 1931-32. Born in Swanton Morley on 2 October 1891 he died at Norwich on 11 October 1963.

SAMUEL JOPLIN HENDERSON   1926-28

The 1927-28 season, in which half-back Henderson had the misfortune to make all but one of his appearances for South Shields, had a high point (he scored in the cheering win at Southampton), and a low point (he was sent off in the FA Cup-tie at Middlesbrough). A native of Willington Quay, Henderson was later on the books of Chelsea and Portsmouth but did not play a first team match for either. Then, after a season at Fulham, he became one of four old South Shields players to join Tunbridge Wells Rangers.

JAMES (Jos) HETHERINGTON   1921-23

Born in Sunderland on 11 April 1892, Jos Hetherington signed for South Shields from a minor Sunderland club, Southwick, and scored on his debut against Sheffield Wednesday in February 1921. He became a regular the following season and his scoring rate against clubs playing the offside game was quite satisfactory. After transferring to Preston North End he had the misfortune to break a leg in his fifth First Division game, against Burnley. Thereafter he made only fleeting appearances for three cities - Lincoln, Durham and Norwich - before leaving the League to join a fourth - Guildford. A disappointing career after a promising start. He died on 6 April 1971 in Nottingham.

HENRY HIGGINBOTHAM   1919-20

Described as a Glaswegian despite being born in Ashfield, New South Wales, Australia in 1894, Higginbotham arrived at South Shields from St. Mirren in 1919. One of football's many 'wanderers' he only played seven games (without scoring) before leaving for Luton Town. He then played for Clapton Orient, a few games for Nelson in their Second Division season (he was sent off for kicking, in the first at Bury) and Reading.

Only at Luton did Higginbotham stay for long, and only there was he a significant goalscorer. He opened the scoring in Luton's comprehensive victory at Horsley Hill in the 1921 FA Cup tie. Henry Higginbotham died in Glasgow on 3 June 1950.

ALEXANDER HIRD   1922-27

Half back Alex Herd signed from Dundee (a club with whom South Shields was always on friendly terms in 1922. He played in approximately one third of South Shields matches during his five years there. Transferring to Charlton Athletic in 1927, he was near ever-present in three seasons.

He remained in Charlton's employment as a trainer until the late 1950's. Born in Montrose on 2 September 1900, he died in South London on 2 January 1988.

EARNEST HOFFMAN   **1919-21**

Born at Hebburn in 1892, goalkeeper Ernie Hoffman had won two amateur International caps, against Sweden in 1913, whilst a Hebburn Argyle player. After guesting for Tottenham Hotspur during the War he signed for South Shields in 1919. His first team appearances were limited after Willis Walker arrived. Rather surprisingly he was transferred to Derby County in 1923 but only made one appearance. He was later with Ashington, Darlington and York City. In the North Eastern League before and after the War he managed Blyth Spartans and the later South Shields FC. Mysteriously Ernie Hoffman seems to have been known by two surnames. Hoffman and Holt and his death on 20 January 1959 is registered under both.

JAMES PRENTICE HOPE   **1928-30**

Born in Wemyss in 1905, James Hope played in the 1927 Scottish Cup Final for East Fife who were beaten by Peter Shevlin's Celtic. All but three of his Third Division (North) appearances in the South Shields defence were in 1928-29. In 1930 he transferred to Chelsea but only made a single First Division appearance.

WILLIAM HOPKINS   **1919-21**

Born at Esh Winning, Co. Durham in 1888 "Pop" Hopkins had made a few First Division appearances for Sunderland before the War. Though approaching the veteran stage (hence his nickname) he made 61 appearances for South Shields after they plucked him from the ashes of the Leeds City club. After assisting Hartlepools United in their first two League seasons he embarked on a career as a trainer with several clubs. Whilst assisting Barnsley in this capacity when they were preparing for a Cup-tie on the Lancashire coast in January 1938 he collapsed, dying a few days later in a Blackpool hospital.

CYRIL HUNTER   **1924-28**

Although born at nearby Pelaw in 1898 Cyril Hunter arrived at South Shields from Brentford in 1924. Although he was definitely one of football's hard men he had a rather soft, cultured voice and a referee once asked if he was a public schoolboy. His antics at Middlesbrough brought him much notoriety but the club thought that his six-month suspension was a harsh one. In 1928 he played in America for Fall River (Massachusetts) but returned to England to play for Lincoln City. Engaged in the furniture trade in later life he died on Tyneside on 16 October 1962.

DAVID HUTCHINSON   **1921-27**

David Hutchinson had been a regular in the Dundee FC half-back line in the 1914-15 season but on returning from War service, and finding it more difficult to maintain his position in his home town team, he accepted a transfer to South Shields where he made 189 appearances in 6 years. The highlight of his South Shields career was in the early part of the 1923-24 season when the South Shields defence seemed almost impregnable.

David Hutchinson

ARCHIBALD JACK   **1919**

A winger born in Grangemouth. Archie Jack had previously played for Falkirk. His seven appearances were all in the first half of the 1919-20 season and his only goal was enough to give South Shields their first away win, at Barnsley.

CHARLES JOHNSON   1919
The initial 1919-20 League season was one in which South Shields seem to have taken on several players for a very short time. Charlie Johnson was described as *"an old South Shields player"* when he helped out briefly.

GEORGE KEENLYSIDE   1919-23
George Keenlyside was signed from Jarrow Croft (his home town club) in 1913 having played briefly for Partick Thistle in 1910-11. He had won high praise in Scotland having scored 3 goals in 7 games and he was a frequent goalscorer in South Shields' two most successful North Eastern League seasons. During the War he served in the Royal Engineers finding time to 'guest' for Barnsley and Nottingham Forest. Though his Second Division career at South Shields was interrupted for a year by injury he was very highly thought of and was granted a testimonial match in April 1922. His last playing season was with Hartlepools United in 1923-24. An engineer by trade George Keenlyside died in South Shields on 18 April 1967 aged 77.

WILLIAM KELLY   1919
A goalkeeper who had little to do on his only appearance against Port Vale on 18 October 1919. An Ulsterman he had played for Linfield and although he was said to have represented Ireland this would seem to refer to Army matches. A year later he was playing for a local colliery team.

ROBERT KENNEDY   1928-30
South Shields were very fortunate to recruit Robert Kennedy from Falkirk though his 53 goals in two seasons there were followed by a mere 24 in the last two Horsley Hill seasons. He kept up the good work at Gateshead before returning to his native Glasgow in 1934 to play for Third Lanark.

HENRY KIRK   1929-30
A wandering scoring forward from Dinnington near Sheffield. He had played for Bristol City, Plymouth Argyle (two spells), Exeter City (two spells), Charlton Athletic, Bath City and New Brighton. South Shields was his last League club in the last Horsley Hill season, then he went back to Bath City.

JOHN PATTERSON KIRKBRIDE   1919-21
'Jacky' Kirkbride was born in Hetton on 14 July 1897. His appearances on the wing attracted favourable comment but he was not retained at the end of 1920-21. He died in Easington on 10 March 1989.

GEORGE LILLYCROP   1919-21

Born on 7 December 1886 in Gosport (all of his relatives having been born in various Army and Navy towns), George Lillycrop was brought up in South Shields. Beginning his professional career with Barnsley he was the leading scorer in three seasons and played in two FA Cup finals. He maintained his high scoring rate with First Division Bolton Wanderers and after the War he offered his services to South Shields. His 17 goals in 44 games for South Shields included four against Blackpool.

He then became the club trainer until the move to Gateshead and was similarly employed there and at Bradford City. In 1938 he became manager of Crewe Alexandra. After the Second World War he was landlord of the Walpole Inn, South Shields (a rendezvous for old footballers) and arranged the annual 'nostalgia' matches at Horsley Hill. He died on 21 January 1962.

George Lillycrop

ALFRED JOHN LITTLEWOOD   1928-30
Littlewood was a half-back. He was born in Esh Winning on 28 January 1902. His eight League appearances for South Shields were in the Third Division (North), after he was signed from Tow Law, and he was among those who moved to Gateshead. He later played for Southport between two spells with Tunbridge Wells Rangers. He remained in the South, playing for a number of small clubs, and died in Strood, Kent, on 3 March 1975.

JOHN LEO LOFTUS   1927-28
Born in Ferryhill, Co. Durham, on 24 January, 1906. John Loftus joined South Shields from Willington. He once scored six goals in a reserve match but his main first team experience was in the relegation season. Nottingham Forest paid a welcome cheque for his services and he was a regular player there and later at Bristol City before bowing out of the League with two games for Gillingham. John Leo Loftus died on 23 October 1992. He had lived in the village of Chilton whose Colliery team it will be recalled played South Shields in the FA Cup in 1926.

ALFRED EDWARD MAITLAND   1919-23
Born in Leith on 8 October 1894, Alf Maitland was rarely absent during his four years at South Shields. Unusually for a Scot he was selected to play for the Football League against the Scottish League. At the very end of his life he was interviewed by the Coalville (Leicestershire) Times and what more eloquent obituary could there be than his own words?

JOHN NICHOLAS MASON   1922
A winger, three of whose four appearances were away from home. Born in North Shields on 17 May 1901 he died there on 25 February 1986.

THOMAS J. MATTHEWSON   1924-30
Born in Gateshead in 1903 Tom Matthewson began his career with Sheffield Wednesday but never made the first team. Transferring to South Shields in 1923 he proceeded to give the club good service for the rest of their years in the town, remaining faithful after relegation. Invariably playing outside-left he often captained the side. He later returned to Sheffield and died there on 19 May 1966.

RANSON MAYCOCK   1928-30
Born in Waterhouses, Co. Durham, the son of a local referee, Ranson Maycock's high scoring with Tow Law in 1927-28 interested several clubs. Struggling South Shields got to him first however, and a goal in his second match at Port Vale helped the club to a rare victory. Relegation was inevitable by then, but Maycock proved to be a fine acquisition being leading scorer in both the Third Division (North) seasons with his best tally being 4 in the 10-1 win over Rotherham. He also scored Gateshead's first goal. Ranson Maycock died in Lanchester Co. Durham on 13 March 1950 aged 44.

GEORGE McCRACKEN   1922
McCracken was a Greenock man who joined South Shields from Port Glasgow Athletic in 1922. His few appearances were in the early part of the 1922-23 season but he failed to dislodge George Keenlyside from his position on the right wing. In 1933 it was reported in a newspaper that he had been injured in an industrial accident locally.

THOMAS McKENNA   1926-27
Born in Stewarton, Ayrshire, on 27 September 1900, McKenna was a goalkeeper who had previously been with Celtic and Fulham. His only season at South Shields was the one in which they started badly, improved, then suffered an alarming number of heavy defeats. The only time McKenna conceded many goals was at Blackpool where he let in six. This was after Allan Taylor had been dropped for doing the same in the previous match.

After a year McKenna returned to London with Charlton Athletic. He then became player/manager of Merthyr Town, relatively successfully, as the season he was there (1928-29) they escaped having to apply for re-election by one point. After a season with Southend United, McKenna played for Portadown in Northern Ireland.

RICHARD MERRITT   **1922**
A winger whose only appearance for South Shields was in a 4-0 defeat at Blackpool. He then toured cathedral cities playing for Durham, Lincoln and York before ending up with Notts County. Born in Shiney Row, Co. Durham, on 22 July 1897 he died in Sunderland in 1978.

JAMES METCALF   **1921-27**
Born in Sunderland on 10 December 1899, Jim Metcalf signed for South Shields from Sunderland Rovers. Making his first appearance in November 1921 at Nottingham Forest he proved to be a dependable half-back clocking up 99 consecutive appearances at one stage. Transferring to Preston North End in 1927 he made only 16 appearances there before ending his playing career with Nelson.

He then returned to Preston North End as a trainer and spent the rest of his working life there (apart from two spells doing the same job at Leicester City), retiring as late as 1968. Away from football he was a church organist at one time. He died in Preston on 20 February 1975.

James Metcalf

JOSEPH THOMAS MITCHELL   **1919**
Goalkeeper Mitchell was among the group of players from the Sheffield area who joined South Shields when they entered the League in 1919. He had much experience with Sheffield United in the First Division and Luton Town in the Southern League but was only called upon once by South Shields. This was in the match at Clapton Orient which was lost 4-0 and was followed by an uncomfortable sea journey. Mitchell later played for Coventry City and Chesterfield. Born in Sheffield on 1 January 1886 he died there on 20 December 1964.

ROBERT P. MURPHY   **1928**
This inside-forward signed for South Sheilds from Unsworth Colliery in 1928 but his only call-up for the first team caused him to miss his Christmas Dinner whilst he made the short trip to Ashington.

JOHN MUSTARD   **1929-30**
Born in Boldon in 1905, John Mustard joined South Shields from Queens Park Rangers in 1929. The fact that he scored in all three meetings with Wrexham in the last Horlsey Hill season was probably the reason the Welsh club signed him. He had two spells at Wrexham and also played for Preston North End, Burnley, Southend United, Crewe Alexandra and New Brighton. He maintained a useful scoring rate at all his clubs.

GEORGE HUMBLE NEILSON   **1928-30**
George Neilson's three League clubs - Durham City, South Shields and Gateshead - have all been consigned to history. Born in Thornley, East Durham, in 1908, Neilson arrived at South Shields in 1928 and was given a chance as a winger in two Second Division matches. Although given a free transfer that Summer, he returned a year later and made 37 appearances as a half back. He proved to be a good servant at Gateshead, remaining with them until the 1938-39 season.

MICHAEL TERENCE O'BRIEN   1920

Half-back O'Brien's three appearances for South Shields in 1920 represented a mere detail in a career which saw playing service with Brentford, Norwich City (twice), Queens Park Rangers, Hull City, Derby County, Walsall and Watford. He found time for a brief and troublesome spell in American soccer and later managed QPR and Ipswich Town. An Irish International born in Kilcock, Co. Down, on 10 August 1893 he died in Uxbridge on 21 September 1940.

JOHN OXBERRY   1919-28

One of the best South Shields players Jack Oxberry was born in Sunderland on 4 April 1901. Making his debut on Boxing Day 1919, Oxberry took some years to establish himself despite consistently high scoring in the reserve side. Unlucky with injuries his only two hat-tricks came against Swansea in the relegation season. His post-South Shields career saw many ups and downs. Helping Blackpool to win promotion to the First Division he then found himself in a team that suffered more heavy defeats than South Shields ever did. Leaving Blackpool he played for Reading then Aldershot.

His career as a trainer began with Gillingham who failed to be re-elected into the League in 1938, and ended with Chelsea who won the League Championship in 1955! Jack Oxberry died in Westminster Hospital on 28 November 1962.

RICHARD PARKER (1)   1920-21

Born in Stockton on Tees on 14 September 1894. Centre-forward Parker began the 1919-20 season with six appearances and two goals for Sunderland. January 1920 found him playing for a Coventry City side who couldn't score goals. His 9 goals in 16 appearances minimised the problem but he was unhappy at Coventry and South Shields paid £1,000 for his services. A debut hat-trick was followed by two more goals in the next eight games but he doesn't seem to have been happy at South Shields either and drifted into North Eastern League football with Wallsend.

He returned to League football scoring many goals for Queens Park Rangers (including 2 against South Shields in the FA Cup), very many, for Millwall and a few for Watford. He died on 1 January 1969 in his native Stockton.

RICHARD PARKER (2)   1925-29

Like Cyril Hunter, Richard ('the second') Parker was a native of Pelaw and they had been team-mates at Brentford where Parker had scored 32 goals in 99 appearances. Hunter recommended his friend to the club and he made his debut at Derby County in November 1925. He maintained his useful scoring rate at Horsley Hill and proved a much better acquisition than his more expensive namesake. In March 1929 he transferred to Merthyr Town who were then managed by former South Shields goalkeeper Thomas McKenna.

WILLIAM KIRTON PARKER   1923-24

A Jarrow man born in 1899, this Parker made 8 appearances in the 1923-24 season, his only goal being enough to earn a point at Port Vale. In the close season he transferred to Swindon Town but never made a League appearance there.

W.J. PATTISON   1924-27

A Durham born full-back who made occasional appearances in the mid-twenties.

CHRISTOPHER J. PEARSON   1925-26

A Sunderland born goalkeeper at various times on the books of West Ham United, Liverpool, Southend United, Derby County, South Shields and Newport County. South Shields was the only one for whom he made League appearances! He proved to be an adequate goalkeeper in his 20 games.

STEVEN S. PEARSON   **1919**

Pearson's single appearance for South Shields was in the first home game against Birmingham. A native of North Shields he had played for Everton in unofficial games just after the War.

JAMES R. PHIZACKLEA   **1926-28**

A full-back born in Barrow on 29 September 1898 whose experience included helping his struggling home town club and playing in the First Division with Preston, from whom South Shields signed him in 1926. A regular over two largely troubled seasons he left the club on less than amicable terms. He died in Braintree, Essex in 1971.

ANDREW RAMAGE   **1927**

Ramage had some scoring experience with Dundee FC and when he arrived at South Shields he scored on his debut against Leeds United on the opening day of the 1927-28 season. It was a mere consolation goal in a 5-1 defeat and he only made two more appearances. He was obviously a big man as a journalist later recalled him having been chased by angry home fans after playing for the reserves at Jarrow. They had mistaken him for Cyril Hunter!

GEORGE TURNBULL REAY   **1923**

Another wandering player, George Reay began with South Shields in 1922-23 season and later played for Reading, Raith Rovers, Bristol Rovers and Coventry City. He was born in East Howden, Co. Durham in February 1903, and died in York on 15 August 1962.

WILLIAM REILLY   **1928-30**

A Scotsman born in Lanark on 24 December 1902. Reilly joined South Shields in 1928 after three years experience of Scottish First Division football with Kilmarnock. A half-back, he missed very few games during the last two Horsley Hill seasons, then put in another season at Gateshead.

EDWARD RICHARDSON   **1920-22**

Richardson who was born in Easington joined South Shields from the colliery team (which also supplied Edward Greenwell). He made 35 appearances over three seasons.

LANCELOT HOLLIDAY RICHARDSON   **1924-26**

A goalkeeper born in Tow Law, Co. Durham, in 1899, Lance Richardson arrived at Horsley Hill from Shildon as understudy to Willis Walker in 1923. After Walker left, Richardson maintained an equally good record rarely conceding more than one goal in a match. He was transferred to Manchester United in 1926 and later played for Reading. He became a rancher in Argentina and died in that country on 22 February 1958.

JOHN GEORGE ('MICK') RIDLEY   **1921-27**

Mick Ridley was born in Bardon Mill, Northumberland on 19 January 1898. After the departure of Warney Cresswell in 1922 he made the left-back position his own and once clocked up a total of 110 consecutive appearances. Sold to Manchester City in September 1927 he helped his new club to win the Second Division championship and played in the First Division for four years. He later played for North Shields. He died in Prudhoe, Northumberland on Christmas Day, 1977.

GEORGE AUSTIN ROBSON   **1920-26**

In the first few years of South Shields' League career the full-backs were usually Cresswell and Maitland. George Robson occasionally filled in when one of them was unavailable. Only after they left for higher things would he establish a regular place with his best season being 1924-25 when he made 29 appearances.

George Robson

George Robson had played for Raith Rovers during the War. In 1926 he was transferred to Southampton but never made a first team appearance there and returning North he played for Achington in their last season in the League. Born in Blyth on 22 April 1897 and died there on 12 March 1984.

JOSEPH WILLIAM ROBSON   **1921-22**
A wing-half who made his debut at Notts County in March 1921 and went on to play 17 matches in all. Born in Sunderland in 1899 he died at Silksworth on 7 November 1961.

ARCHIBALD ROE   **1919**
Archie Roe only played in South Shields' first two League games but brought the house down with his last minute winner against Birmingham. Although a man of many subsequent clubs - Birmingham, Gillingham, Arsenal, Lincoln, Rotherham - that wet Monday night in South Shields must have remained a favourite memory. Born in Hull on 9 December 1893 he was a Sheffield publican at the time of his death which occurred on 17 October 1947, whilst he was visiting his daughter in Wigan.

GEORGE SCOTT   **1927-29**
If a table was ever to be compiled measuring the success of players careers by the number of times they finished on the winning or losing side George Scott would be near the foot of it.
His second League game for South Shields was in the 8-2 defeat at Darlington in March 1927 and by the end of the following season he had played on the winning side in only 5 of his 39 games. Transferring to Newcastle United for £1,250 in April 1929 he found the Magpies to be struggling against relegation. Then it was Gillingham who had to apply for re-election. Still there was the odd highlight with Scott scoring once in South Shields' 5-3 win at Southampton and twice in the 10-1 victory over Rotherham. George Scott was born in Blackhill, Co. Durham.

JOHN SCOTT   **1928-30**
Half-back John Scott was born in 1905 in the Durham village of Hamsterley Colliery. He began his career with Oldham Athletic but only made his League debut after transferring to South Shields in 1928. Part of the mass migration to Redheugh Park he remained with Gateshead until 1934. Transferring to Crewe he was still playing on the last day of the 1938-39 season.

JOSEPH SCOTT   **1928**
Joe Scott had played for Darlington for three seasons before arriving at South Shields in 1928. His only League appearances were in the Christmas matches against Ashington and he was given a free transfer at the end of the season. Born in Newcastle.

WALTER SCOTT   **1921**
Walter Scott arrived from Blyth Spartans and later moved on to Ashington. He has often been confused with William Scott (1893 - 1972) who although employed by South Shields as a trainer did not make any Football League appearances; he later managed Preston North End.

PETER SHEVLIN   **1927-29**
Shevlin's goalkeeping career scaled the heights with Celtic, with whom he won a championship and a Cup winners medal, and it plumbed the depths with the woeful defensive records of South Shields and Nelson. His arrival at South Shields in 1927 was seen as a feather in the cap of new manager Ernie Douglas. Despite conceding so many, Shevlin's performances were highly praised and often saved the side from heavier defeats.

Peter Shevlin

After Third Division (North) experience with South Shields and Nelson he returned to Scotland to play for Hamilton Academicals and Albion Rovers. Peter Shevlin was born in Wishaw on 18 November 1905 and died in Manchester on 10 October 1948.

ERNEST SIMMS   1922-24

Ernie Simms was not born in South Shields as often stated but in the mining village of Murton on 23 July 1891. Arriving at Luton Town (via Barnsley) in 1913. Simms scored prolifically for the Hatters in two divisions of the Southern League and was the Third Division (South)'s leading scorer when South Shields signed him.

His scoring touch deserted him at South Shields but returned briefly when he was transferred to Stockport County, scoring a rapid hat-trick - against South Shields. He preferred playing against weaker defences netting 36 in 20 games on an FA tour of Australia in 1925, and later resumed his high scoring ways with Scunthorpe United and York City, both of whom were then in the Midland League. He had won an England Cap (vs Wales) whilst at Luton. Returning to live in Luton he died there on 11 October 1971.

THOMAS MACKIE SINCLAIR   1928-30

Born in Alva, Scotland, Sinclair had made 2 appearances for Celtic before arriving at Horsley Hill in the summer of 1928. Evidently a dependable full-back he was an ever-present in both of the Third Division (North) seasons and went on to give good service to Gateshead after the move.

ARTHUR SMITH   1919-20

A local youth from Tyne Dock who had played for a team called Wenlock. Although his career only consisted of four consecutive League matches, and two FA Cup games against Liverpool, it would seem to have been an enjoyable one. A newspaper described his debut against Stockport County as *"brilliant"*. Then there was the greatest of all South Shields games - the 7-1 victory over Hull City on 3 January 1920.

Ernest Simms

GEORGE SMITH   1919

On 6 December 1919 South Shields found themselves without a right-winger for the home game with Leicester City. The reserves arrived at West Stanley to be met by a taxi to transport George Smith back to Horsley Hill at high speed. Arriving in the nick of time to find the directors *"crying for very joy"* and Jack Tinn *"almost in hysterics"*, Smith rewarded their faith in him by scoring after 15 minutes. It proved to be his only goal for the club in his nine appearances. The following season he made nine appearances for Brentford (including their first Football League match at Exeter) and was given a free transfer.

JOHN W. SMITH   1919-27

One of the famous footballing clan from nearby Whitburn (born 28 October 1898). ' Jack' Smith was three times leading scorer in his seven years with the club. Jack Tinn took him to Portsmouth in 1927 where he scored 61 goals in 261 games, played in 2 Cup Finals, and was capped three times for England. He ended his career with Bournemouth and died in 1977.

WILLIAM H. SMITH   1927

A much younger brother of Jack, William was born on 9 June 1909. Although his first League season as a South Shields player involved appearing mostly in a losing side, he followed Jack to Portsmouth where he established himself as a near ever-present right-back and played in the FA Cup Final in 1934. He bowed out with Stockport County.

JOHN ROBERT SOULSBY   1920

This player's only appearance was at Hull in January 1920. He later played in the North Eastern League for Darlington and Blyth Spartans. He died in North Shields on 3 July 1940 aged 44.

PAUL STANNARD   1924

In a reversal of the far more usual procedure a leading North Eastern club signed a player from a minor club in the Midlands when Sunderland signed Paul Stannard from Tamworth Castle in May 1921. After only 13 League appearances with Sunderland he transferred to South Shields making a scoring debut against Port Vale on New Years Day of 1924. He left for Carlisle United in the following close season and later played for Jarrow. Paul Stannard was born in Warwickshire on 17 January 1895, and died in Birmingham on 24 November 1982.

JAMES STEVENSON   1927-29

Scotsmen signed by South Shields tended to make little impression and left soon after their arrival, but Jimmy Stevenson was an exception. Arriving from Third Lanark he made a scoring debut in February 1927 but must have thought his efforts wasted over the next year or so. Of the nine Second Division matches in which he scored, 7 were lost and 2 drawn. To make things worse he was sent off in the FA Cup-tie at Middlesbrough.

The goals he scored in the lower divisions were to much better effect and included a hat-trick against Rochdale. He left to play for Bradford City, Aldershot, and eventually Stockport County, in whose employment he remained long after his playing days were over. He was born in New Mains, Lanarkshire, on 10 November 1903, and died in Stockport on 5 November 1973.

EDWARD STOTHARD   1919-22

Stothard was a native of Benwell, Newcastle, and signed for South Shields from North Eastern League club Scotswood. He played in the first League game at Fulham and made occasional appearances over the next three seasons.

JAMES H. TALBOT   1928-30

Winger Talbot was signed from the Craghead club after a good performance against South Shields Reserves in 1928. A native of Penshaw, Sunderland, he made many appearances over the next two seasons, all of his goals coming in the 1929-30 season. He then moved to Gateshead with the club.

Edward Stothard

ALBERT TAYLOR   1929-30

A winger from Bedlington who showed early promise which never materialised. Stan Seymour wrote that he was *"delighted with Taylor"* in his second match at York in November 1929. Two months later the club rejected a large offer for him. Gateshead, however, sold him to Chelsea in 1931 but he never made the first team and had to be content with 53 appearances for Bristol Rovers and a few for Lincoln City and Gillingham.

ALLAN TAYLOR   1926-29

A goalkeeper from North Shields (born there on 1 December 1905), Taylor had made a single First Division appearance for Newcastle United. As South Shields struggled in the Second Division, Taylor's misfortunes included conceding eight goals at Darlington and seven at Preston. He made sporadic appearances for Tottenham Hotspur in the thirties though with limited success and Wolves, Arsenal and Leicester all scored six against him in another relegation season. There was more struggle in his last League season with Hartlepools United. Allan Taylor died at Whitley Bay on 11 April 1981.

WILLIAM J. THIRLAWAY   1925-26

Bill Thirlaway travelled the League circuit with six different clubs in the twenties. A regular with West Ham United in 1921-22 he fell out of favour there and played Third Division (South) games for Southend United and Luton Town before arriving at Horsley Hill in the close season of 1925. The following season was a good one to be at South Shields (despite falling gates) and one of his goals was in the memorable victory at Preston. Then it was back on the train to Birmingham, Cardiff City and (oddly) Tunbridge Wells Rangers. In 1931 a journalist recalled that Thirlaway was *"a popular little player with the Horsley Hill crowd"* but less popular with other players and officials. Born in New Washington on 1 October 1896, Bill Thirlaway died in 1983.

NORMAN THOMPSON   1923-25

Norman Thompson was born at Forest Hall, Newcastle, on 5 September 1900. He made his South Shields debut in the 1922-23 season but it took him two years to establish himself as a first team player despite being leading scorer for the reserve side. The highlight of his career was scoring the winning goal in the fine match against Derby County on Good Friday 1925. He transferred to Middlesbrough shortly afterwards but only played a few games for them as was also the case with his two later clubs, Barnsley and Nottingham Forest.

THOMAS SMITH TRAYNOR   1919-20

Tommy Traynor had played for South Shields before the War. His post-War career was mostly as a reserve though he did play in the first League match at Fulham. He left in 1921 to join Ebbw Vale. He had won more distinction in another sphere having been mentioned in despatches for bravery on the Somme on 21 March 1918. Born in South Shields on 23 December 1894, he died in Basingstoke on 3 March 1985.

ALEXANDER E. TROTTER   1924-27

Although a local man from Jarrow, Alex Trotter had played for Raith Rovers, Dumbarton and Leicester City before joining South Shields in 1924. Ever-present on the right wing in 1925-26, Trotter had escaped to Port Vale shortly before the awful 1927-28 season began.

ROBERT A. TURNBULL   1928-30

Turnbull, a native of Cornsay, Co. Durham, made his debut at right-back in a 4-1 defeat at Blackpool on 21 April 1928. All his other appearances for South Shields were in the Third Division (North). After assisting Gateshead for three years he transferred to Millwall making 88 appearances between 1933-36.

WILLIS WALKER   1919-24

Although born in Gosforth on 24 November 1892 goalkeeper Willis Walker lived in Yorkshire most of his life. His first club was Sheffield United (though his only appearances were for the cricket section of the club), Doncaster Rovers (who were struggling in the Midland League), and Leeds City for whom he made his debut in February 1915. South Shields were successful in their bid for him in the 1919 auction of Leeds City players.

In 199 appearances he kept a clean sheet in 80 matches and only conceded one goal in each of 70 other games. He had an impressive record in saving penalties. His last season was spent with Bradford (Park Avenue). Willis Walker was also well known as a Nottinghamshire County cricketer from 1913 to 1937. His death at the age of 99 on 3 December 1991 caused a newspaper to note that he had been the oldest surviving County player.

THOMAS WILKINSON   1927
A local boy from Willington Quay whose five games on the wing resulted in three draws and two heavy defeats.

HARRY WILSON   1919-28
The most versatile of the South Shields players, Harry Wilson played in full-back, half-back and forward positions. 15 of his 19 goals were scored the 1925-26 season when he regularly played at centre-forward.

Born in nearby Marsden, his career parallels that of Johnny Oxberry. Both played for South Shields in all nine Second Division seasons, both were transferred to Blackpool, and both ended their days as trainers of First Division clubs. Harry Wilson could boast of involvement with Stanley Matthews and Blackpool's famous FA Cup victory of 1953, whilst Oxberry could celebrate Chelsea's League Championship season and the later emergence of Jimmy Greaves.

HENRY WOODS   1919-22
One of South Shields' star forwards, Woods was born in St. Helens, Lancashire, on 12 March 1890. He joined the club from Norwich City and played in the first League match at Fulham. Among the leading scorers in his three seasons at the club he was sold to Newcastle in 1922. There his first team appearances were limited but after transferring to Arsenal he was leading scorer in 2 consecutive seasons. He later played for Luton Town and returned to the district to join North Shields.

ERNEST YOUNG   1919-20
Ernie Young made 10 appearances at centre-forward in the first League season. He played in the first home game against Birmingham and later in the season he scored twice against both Nottingham Forest and Rotherham County. Not wishing to devote himself to playing full-time, and prevented by other employment from making long journeys regularly, Young played mostly in the reserve side in which he was leading scorer. Durham City were pleased to secure his services the following season. He was born in Sunderland in 1892 and died in 1962.

ROBERT YOUNG   1921
Born in Catrine, Ayrshire in 1894, Robert Young had much Scottish League experience with Queens Park, Albion Rovers and Ayr United. His only game for South Shields was on the right-wing in a goalless home draw with Nottingham Forest.

South Shields Team Groups

1919/20 Season
Back: Dodds (Director), Gibbon, Hoffman, Rigby (Director)
Middle: Tinn (Sec/Manager), Maitland, Hampson, Frith, Stothard, Cresswell, Smith
Front: Keenlyside, Woods, Bell, Wilson, Higginbotham

1921/22 Season
Back: Maidment, Bouran, Maitland, Cresswell, Walker, G.Robson, R.Young, W.Young, Woods, Keenlyside
Second Row:: Rutherford, Robinson, Ormston, J.Robson, Wilson, Hutchison,
Metcalfe, Doherty, Greenwell, Hoffman, Mann
Third Row: Stothard, Charlton, Ridley, Casson, Tinn (Sec/Manager), Hetherington, Hawes, Smith, Scott
Front: Miles (Trainer), Johnston, Oxberry, Hardy, Bell, Lillycrop (Asst.Train.),

1923/24 Season
Back: Ridley, Matthewson, R.Henderson, Walker, Crown, Thompson, Robson, J.Henderson.
Middle: Lillycrop (Trainer), Chape, Wilson, Hird, Hardy, Hutchison,
Stothard, Metcalf, Wynter (Asst.Trainer).
Front: Smith, Oxberry, Bolam, Hetherington, Simms, Greenwell, Brown, Parker, Guyan.

1924/25 Season
Back: Metcalf, Ridley, Hunter, Richardson, Robson, Hutchison, Lillycrop (Trainer)
Front: Matthewson, Smith, Oxberry, Thonpson, Trotter,

1928/29 Season
Back:Percy (Asst.Trainer), Hope, Sinclair, Turner,
Shevlin, Taylor, Creighton, Grenyer, Lillycrop (Trainer)
Middle: Matthewson, Loftus, Kennedy, Maycock,
Douglass (Sec/Manager), Parker, Stevenson, Reilly, G.Scott
Front: Davies, Littlewood, Neilson, J.Scott, Dunn

South Shields' Record Against other Football League Clubs 1919-1930

South Shields played 58 clubs during their League career and recorded at least one victory against 52 of them, the exceptions being Cardiff City, Huddersfield Town, Tottenham Hotspur and West Bromwich Albion in the Second Division, plus New Brighton and Wigan Borough in the Third Division (North). On the other hand 54 clubs beat South Shields at least once with only Ashington, Crewe Alexandra, Halifax Town and York City - all of the Third Division (North) - failing to do so. The "double" was accomplished against 20 clubs - twice against Coventry City, Fulham, Halifax Town, Nelson and Southampton. 24 clubs took maximum League points against South Shields with Blackpool, Manchester United, New Brighton, Stockport County and Wolverhampton Wanderers all accomplishing the "double" twice. Rotherham's record at Horsley Hill is not quite as bad as South Shields' record at Darlington in terms of goals conceded per game.

Team	H-W	H-D	H-L	H-F	H-A	A-W	A-D	A-L	A-F	A-A
Accrington Stanley	1	1	0	5	2	1	0	1	2	3
Ashington	0	1	0	0	0	1	0	0	3	1
Barnsley	7	2	0	27	7	1	2	6	5	19
Barrow	1	1	0	4	2	0	1	1	4	2
Birmingham	2	0	0	4	0	0	1	1	1	5
Blackpool	5	2	2	19	12	1	1	7	8	27
Bradford	1	0	0	1	0	0	0	1	0	1
Bradford City	1	4	1	6	7	1	1	4	4	9
Bristol City	1	2	2	4	6	1	1	3	5	9
Bury	2	2	1	4	3	1	0	4	2	5
Cardiff City	0	0	1	0	1	0	0	1	0	1
Carlisle United	2	0	0	10	2	0	0	2	1	9
Chelsea	2	2	0	8	3	0	2	2	2	11
Chesterfield	2	0	0	9	4	1	0	1	4	4
Clapton Orient	6	3	0	17	5	2	3	4	5	12
Coventry City	5	1	0	15	5	3	1	2	5	3
Crewe Alexandra	2	0	0	4	0	1	1	0	7	3
Crystal Palace	2	2	0	6	2	1	2	1	3	3
Darlington	1	1	2	7	10	0	1	3	8	22
Derby County	4	1	0	10	4	1	1	3	3	9
Doncaster Rovers	2	0	0	3	1	0	0	2	1	3
Fulham	8	1	0	19	5	2	3	4	8	13
Grimsby Town	2	0	1	6	4	0	1	2	3	8
Halifax Town	2	0	0	3	1	2	0	0	4	0
Hartlepools United	0	1	1	4	6	1	0	1	6	2
Huddersfield Town	0	0	1	1	2	0	1	0	2	2
Hull City	5	2	2	15	6	3	1	5	7	11
Leeds United	2	0	3	6	8	2	1	2	4	6
Leicester City	4	1	1	11	7	0	2	4	2	11
York City	1	0	0	4	1	0	1	0	2	2

Team	H-W	H-D	H-L	H-F	H-A	A-W	A-D	A-L	A-F	A-A
Lincoln City	2	1	0	6	3	0	2	1	3	8
Manchester City	0	1	1	2	3	1	0	1	2	4
Manchester United	1	0	2	2	5	0	1	2	1	5
Middlesbrough	0	2	1	2	3	1	1	1	3	7
Nelson	3	0	0	8	3	2	0	1	3	1
New Brighton	0	0	2	1	4	0	0	2	1	5
Notts County	3	1	1	9	3	0	0	5	2	14
Nottingham Forest	2	2	2	12	9	1	1	4	7	17
Oldham Athletic	2	2	1	6	4	0	1	4	5	9
Portsmouth	2	0	1	6	3	0	1	2	3	6
Port Vale	5	3	2	25	12	2	3	5	9	17
Preston North End	0	2	1	4	5	1	0	2	6	11
Reading	1	1	0	3	0	0	0	2	2	7
Rochdale	1	1	0	7	4	1	0	1	2	3
Rotherham Co./Utd.	6	0	0	26	3	1	2	3	8	10
Sheffield Wed.	0	4	2	5	7	2	1	3	5	9
Southampton	2	2	2	7	6	3	2	1	11	10
Southport	2	0	0	8	0	0	0	2	1	7
Stockport County	5	0	3	18	11	0	3	5	5	18
Stoke/City	3	3	1	16	8	1	4	2	3	5
Swansea Town	2	0	1	6	3	1	0	2	5	9
Tottenham Hotspur	0	0	1	0	3	0	0	1	0	2
Tranmere Rovers	1	0	1	5	6	0	0	2	0	7
West Bromwich Alb.	0	0	1	2	3	0	0	1	0	3
West Ham United	2	2	0	4	0	0	1	3	2	5
Wigan Borough	0	2	0	4	4	0	1	1	1	5
Wolverhampton W.	1	4	3	11	13	0	1	7	4	15
Wrexham	1	1	0	4	3	1	0	1	3	2

	W	D	L	F	A	W	D	L	F	A
TOTAL	120	64	47	441	247	45	53	133	208	437

Statistics Notes:

The pages that follow (pages 80-90) contain the full statistical record of the club's Football League career and is generally self-explanatory: The first column is the League match number or FA Cup round; the second column contains the fixture date, and the third column the opposition (upper case - capitals - are home matches, and lower case are games played away); the fourth column is the match result (South Shields score first), followed by the names of goalscorers - 'pen' is a goal scored from a penalty, and 'og' is an own goal with the opposition player's name; where known, official attendances follow. The rest of the table contains the team line-ups; whilst shirt numbering was not introduced until much later, the normal accepted playing positions are included, i.e. 1 = goalkeeper, 2 = right back, 6 = left-half, 8 = inside right, etc. The summaries below the line-ups refer to total League appearances and goals scored by that player.

1919-20 9th in Division 2

Average (Home) Attendance: 14975 (based on estimates)

#	Date	Opposition	Score	Scorers	Hoffman	Cresswell	Maitland	Stothard	Frith	Traynor	Higginbotham	Roe	Burkinshaw	Woods	Keenlyside	Young	Hampson	Bell	Wilson	Smith J.W.	Smith G.	Jack	Walker	Johnson	Hopkins	Charlton	Oxberry	Smith A.	Robson	O'Brien	Kirkbridge	Lillycrop	Dreyer
1	Aug 30	Fulham	0-1		1	2	3	4	5	6	7	8	9	10																			
2	Sep 1	BIRMINGHAM	1-1	Roe	1	2	3	4	5		7	8		10	9																		
3	6	FULHAM	2-0	Frith, Bell	1	2	3	4	5			8	10			6	9																
4	10	Birmingham	0-4		1	2	3	4	5		7			10			4	9	8														
5	13	Hottenham Hotspur	0-2		1	2	3	4	5		7			10			6		8	9													
6	20	TOTTENHAM HOTSPUR	0-3		1	2	3	4	5					10			6	9	8						7								
7	27	Clapton Orient	0-4			2		4	5	6				10			3	9		8	7												
8	Oct 4	CLAPTON ORIENT	2-0	Dreyer, Lillycrop		2		4						10			6			8	7	11		3							9	5
9	18	PORT VALE	2-0	J.W.Smith(2,1pen)		2		4						10			6			8	7	11		3							9	5
10	25	Bury	1-2	Woods		2		4			7			10			6			8	11		1	3	5						9	
11	Nov 1	BURY	0-0			2		4			7			10			6			8	11		1	3	5						9	
12	8	Nottingham Forest	0-0			2	3	4						10			6			8	7	11	1		5						9	
13	10	Port Vale	0-1			2	3		4					10			6			8	7	11	1		5	9						
14	15	NOTTINGHAM FOREST	5-2	J.W.Smith, Young(2), Woods, Flynn		2	3		4					10		9	6			8		1			5	7							
15	22	Leicester City	0-0			2	3		4					10		9	6			8	11	1			5	7							
16	29	LEICESTER CITY	2-0	J.W.Smith, G.Smith		2	3							10		9	6			8	11	1			5	7							4
17	Dec 6	Barnsley	1-0	Jack		2	3							10		9	6			8	11	1			5	7							4
18	13	BARNSLEY	0-0			2	3							10		9	6			8	11	1			5	7							4
19	20	Stockport County	0-1			2	3	4	6					10	9					8		1				7							5
20	26	Wolverhampton W.	0-0			2	3	4	6					10						8		1				7	9						5
21	27	STOCKPORT COUNTY	3-2	Maitland, J.W.Smith, Charlton		2	3	5	6											8		1				7	10	11				9	4
22	Jan 1	WOLVERHAMPTON W.	0-0				2	5												8		1				7	10	11	3			9	4
23	3	HULL CITY	7-1	Dreyer, Charlton(3), J.S.Smith(2) *			2		6											8		1			5	7	10	11	3			9	4
24	17	Hull City	0-3			2			6					8								1			5	7	10	11	3	4			
25	24	Coventry City	1-1	Oxberry		2	3		6					8						10		1			5	7	9					11	4
26	31	COVENTRY CITY	1-0	J.W.Smith		2	3		6					8						10		1			5	7	9					11	4
27	Feb 7	Huddersfield Town	2-2	Lillycrop, Woods		2	3		6					10						8		1			5	7						11	4
28	14	HUDDERSFIELD TOWN	1-2	J.W.Smith		2	3		6					10						8		1			5	7						11	4
29	21	Blackpool	3-0	Charlton, Woods(2)		2	3							10		6				8		1			5	7						11	4
30	28	BLACKPOOL	6-0	Charlton, J.W.Smith, Lillicrop(4)		2	3							10		6				8		1			5	7						11	4
31	Mar 10	BRISTOL CITY	0-2			2	3							10		6				8		1			5	7						11	4
32	13	Bristol City	1-3	Woods		2	3							10		6				8		1				7			2			11	4
33	20	WEST HAM UNITED	3-0	J.W.Smith, Lillycrop(2)		2	3			4				10		6				8		1				7						11	5
34	27	West Ham United	0-1			2	3			4				10		6				8		1				7						11	5
35	Apr 2	LINCOLN CITY	2-2	Charlton, Woods		2	3							10		6				8		1			5	7						11	4
36	3	ROTHERHAM COUNTY	6-2	J.W.Smith(2),Young(2),Charlton,Woods			3							10	9	6				8		1			5	7			2			11	4
37	5	Lincoln City	1-1	J.W.Smith											9	3				8		1			5	7	10		2	6	11		4
38	10	Rotherham County	0-1				3							10	8	6				8		1			5	7			2			11	4
39	17	STOKE	2-2	Oxberry, Lillycrop			3							10		6						1			5	7	8		2			11	4
40	24	Stoke	0-0				3							10						8		1			5	7			2	6	11	9	4
41	26	GRIMSBY TOWN	2-0	Lillycrop, Woods	1		3							10		6				8		1			5	7			2			9	4
42	May 1	Grimsby Town	1-3	J.W.Smith	1	2	3							10						8		1			5						11	9	4

Additional players: Mitchell 7/1, Browning 8/1, Kelly 9/1
Brayson 19,20/11, Richardson 41/11, 42/7, Pearson 2/6
Flynn 14/11 (1 goal), Davidson 22/6, Soulsby 24/9.   * additional goalscorer - Eddleston (og)

| | | | | | 8 | 34 | 35 | 16 | 19 | 4 | 7 | 2 | 2 | 38 | 7 | 10 | 29 | 4 | 3 | 34 | 8 | 7 | 31 | 4 | 26 | 30 | 9 | 4 | 10 | 3 | 17 | 22 | 28 |
| | | | | | | | | | | | | | 1 | | | 1 | | | | 9 | | 4 | | 1 | | | 15 | 1 | 1 | | 8 | 2 | | | 10 | 2 |

1 Own Goal

F.A. Cup

	Date	Opposition	Score	Att	Cresswell	Maitland	Frith	Woods	Young	Wilson	Jack	Smith A.	Charlton	Oxberry	Robson	Lillycrop	Dreyer
1R	Jan 10	LIVERPOOL	1-1	Woods	7790	2	3	6		9		8		1	5	7	10	11		4
1Rr	14	Liverpool	0-2		39000	2	3	6		8	9		1	5	7	10	11		4

1919/20 Football League Division 2

		P	W	D	L	F	A	W	D	L	F	A	F	A	Pts
				Home						Away					
1	Tottenham Hotspur	42	19	2	0	60	11	13	4	4	42	21	102	32	70
2	Huddersfield Town	42	16	4	1	58	13	12	4	5	39	25	97	38	64
3	Birmingham	42	14	3	4	54	16	10	5	6	31	18	85	34	56
4	Blackpool	42	13	4	4	40	18	8	6	7	25	29	65	47	52
5	Bury	42	14	4	3	35	15	6	4	11	25	29	60	44	48
6	Fulham	42	11	6	4	36	18	8	3	10	25	32	61	50	47
7	West Ham United	42	14	3	4	34	14	5	6	10	13	26	47	40	47
8	Bristol City	42	9	9	3	30	18	4	8	9	16	25	46	43	43
9	SOUTH SHIELDS	42	13	5	3	47	18	2	7	12	11	30	58	48	42
10	Stoke	42	13	3	5	37	15	5	3	13	23	39	60	54	42
11	Hull City	42	13	4	4	53	23	5	2	14	25	49	78	72	42
12	Barnsley	42	9	5	7	41	28	6	5	10	20	27	61	55	40
13	Port Vale	42	11	3	7	35	27	5	5	11	24	35	59	62	40
14	Leicester City	42	8	6	7	26	29	7	4	10	15	32	41	61	40
15	Clapton Orient	42	14	3	4	34	17	2	3	16	17	42	51	59	38
16	Stockport County	42	11	4	6	34	24	3	5	13	18	37	52	61	37
17	Rotherham County	42	10	4	7	32	27	3	4	14	19	56	51	83	34
18	Nottingham Forest	42	9	4	8	23	22	2	5	14	20	51	43	73	31
19	Wolverhampton W.	42	8	4	9	41	32	2	6	13	14	48	55	80	30
20	Coventry City	42	7	7	7	20	26	2	4	15	15	47	35	73	29
21	Lincoln City	42	8	6	7	27	30	1	3	17	17	71	44	101	27
22	Grimsby Town	42	8	4	9	23	24	2	1	18	11	51	34	75	25

1920-21 8th in Division 2

Average (Home) Attendance: 16450 (based on estimates)

#	Date		Opponent	Score	Scorers	Walker	Cresswell	Maitland	Dreyer	Hopkins	Hampson	Bainbridge	Woods	Lillycrop	Hawes	Richardson	Wilson	Kirkbride	Charlton	Smith	Parker	Keenlyside	Metcalf	Donald	Hoffman	Hetherington	Robson G	Robson J.W.	Ridley	Oxberry	Stothard	Carruthers	Greenwell
1	Aug 28		BIRMINGHAM	3-0	Lillycrop, Hawes(2)	1	2	3	4	5	6	7	8	9	10	11																	
2	Sep 1		Leeds United	2-1	Woods(2)	1	2	3	4	5	6	7	8	9	10	11																	
3		4	Birmingham	1-1	Woods(2)	1	2	3	4	5	6	7	8	9	10	11																	
4		8	LEEDS UNITED	3-0	Bainbridge, Hawes(2)	1	2	3	4	5	6	7	8	9	10	11																	
5		11	BARNSLEY	3-2	Hawes(2), Richardson	1	2	3	4	5	6	7	8		10	11	9																
6		18	Barnsley	1-1	Woods	1	2	3	4	5	6	7	8		10		9	11															
7		25	ROTHERHAM CO.	1-0	Hawes	1	2	3	4	5	6	7	8	9	10	11																	
8	Oct 2		Rotherham Co.	4-5	Hopkins, Wilson, Hawes(2)	1	2	3	4	5	6	7	8		10		9	11															
9		9	COVENTRY CITY	4-1	Bainbridge(2), Wood, Charlton	1	2	3	4	5	6	7	8		10			11	9														
10		16	Coventry City	0-1		1	2	3	4	5	6	7	8		10			11		9													
11		23	PORT VALE	6-1	Woods, Parker(3,1pen), Hawes(2)	1	2	3	4	5	6		8		10						7		9	11									
12		30	Port Vale	2-0	Charlton, Woods	1	2	3	4	5	6		8		10						7		9	11									
13	Nov 6		NOTTINGHAM FOREST	0-1		1	2	3	4	5	6		8		10						7		9	11									
14		13	Nottingham Forest	2-1	Woods(2)	1	2	3	4	5			8		10			11			9	7	6										
15		20	HULL CITY	0-0		1	2	3	4	5			8		10	11					7	9	6										
16		27	Hull City	2-0	Parker, Kirkbride	1	2	3	4	5			8		10			11			7	9	6										
17	Dec 4		WOLVERHAMPTON W.	1-2	Parker	1	2	3	4	5	6		8		10			11	7		9												
18		11	Wolverhampton W.	0-3		1	2	3	4	5	6		8	9	10							7	11										
19		18	Stockport County	0-0		1	2	3	4	5	6		8		10						7	9	11										
20		25	Bury	0-1		1	2	3	4	5	6		8	9							7	10	11									
21		27	BURY	2-0	Hampson(2)	1	2	3	4	5	6		8	9	10						7		11										
22	Jan 1		STOCKPORT CO.	3-1	Hopkins, Lillycrop, Hawes	1	2	3		5	6		8	9	10						7	4	11										
23		15	STOKE	1-1	Hawes	1	2	3		5	6		8	9	10	11					7	4											
24		22	Stoke	0-0			2	3	6	5			8		10					9	7	4	11	1									
25	Feb 2		CLAPTON ORIENT	3-0	Lillycrop(2), Hawes	1	2	3		5				9	10	4					7	6	11		8								
26		5	Clapton Orient	0-1		1	2	3		5				9	10	4					7	6	11		8								
27		12	SHEFFIELD WED.	2-3	Hetherington, Hawes	1	2	3		5				9	10	4			7			6	11			8							
28		19	Sheffield Wed.	1-1	Hawes		2			5				9	10	4			7	8		6	11	1			3						
29		26	NOTTS COUNTY	1-0	Lillycrop		2		4	5				9	10			8	7				11	1			3	6					
30	Mar 5		Notts County	0-2			2	3	4	5			8			9		10	11	8	7			1				6					
31		12	BLACKPOOL	1-0	Woods		2		6	5			8	9	10	11	4				7			1				3					
32		19	Blackpool	2-3	Keenlyside, Woods		2		6	5			8	9	10	11	4				7			1				3					
33		25	BRISTOL CITY	0-0			2							9	10	8	4				7			1				3					
34		26	Leicester City	0-2			2			6				5	8	10	11	4			7			1				3		9			
35		28	Bristol City	2-4	Oxberry, Richardson		4					5		8	9		11				7			1				3	6	2	10		
36	Apr 2		LEICESTER CITY	4-3	Keenlyside(2), Oxberry, Richardson		2			4	5			8	9			11			7			1				3	6	10			
37		9	Cardiff City	0-1			2							8	10	11	4				7	6		1				3		9	5		
38		16	CARDIFF CITY	0-1			2						8	9	10	11	4				7	6		1				3			5		
39		23	Fulham	0-0		1	2						8		10		4				7	6	11					3		9	5		
40		30	FULHAM	3-0	Woods(2), Carruthers	1	2						8		10		4					6	11					3				5	9
41	May 2		West Ham United	1-2	Maitland	1	2	9					7		8		4					6						3				5	10
42		7	WEST HAM UNITED	0-0		1	2						7	8	10			11				4	11				3	6				5	9
						30	39	32	30	35	21	13	36	22	38	17	18	8	13	7	9	22	15	10	12	1	14	5	1	5	6	2	1
								1		2	2	3	13	5	16	3	1	1	2		5	3			1				2		1	

F.A. Cup

	Date	Opponent	Score		Att	Walker	Cresswell	Maitland	Dreyer	Hopkins	Hampson	Bainbridge	Woods	Lillycrop	Hawes	Richardson	Wilson	Kirkbride	Charlton	Smith	Parker	Keenlyside	Metcalf	Donald	Hoffman
1R	Jan 8	PORTSMOUTH	3-0	Maitland(pen), Hawes, Potts (OG)	15510	1	2	3		5	6		8	9	10						7	4	11		
2R		29	Luton Town	0-4		21003	1	2	3		5	6			10					8	9	7	4	11		

1920/21 Football League Division 2

		P	W	D	L	F	A	W	D	L	F	A	F	A	Pts
				Home						Away					
1	Birmingham	42	16	4	1	55	13	8	6	7	24	25	79	38	58
2	Cardiff City	42	13	5	3	27	9	11	5	5	32	23	59	32	58
3	Bristol City	42	14	3	4	35	12	5	10	6	14	17	49	29	51
4	Blackpool	42	12	3	6	32	19	8	7	6	22	23	54	42	50
5	West Ham United	42	13	5	3	38	11	6	5	10	13	19	51	30	48
6	Notts County	42	12	5	4	36	17	6	6	9	19	23	55	40	47
7	Clapton Orient	42	13	6	2	31	9	3	7	11	12	33	43	42	45
8	SOUTH SHIELDS	42	13	4	4	41	16	4	6	11	20	30	61	46	44
9	Fulham	42	14	4	3	33	12	2	6	13	10	35	43	47	42
10	Sheffield Wed.	42	9	7	5	31	14	6	4	11	17	34	48	48	41
11	Bury	42	10	8	3	29	13	5	2	14	16	36	45	49	40
12	Leicester City	42	10	8	3	26	11	2	8	11	13	35	39	46	40
13	Hull City	42	7	10	4	24	18	3	10	8	19	35	43	53	40
14	Leeds United	42	11	5	5	30	14	3	5	13	10	31	40	45	38
15	Wolverhampton W.	42	11	4	6	34	24	5	2	14	15	42	49	66	38
16	Barnsley	42	9	9	10	2	31	17	1	6	14	17	33	48	50	36
17	Port Vale	42	7	6	8	28	19	4	8	9	15	30	43	49	36
18	Nottingham Forest	42	9	6	6	37	26	3	6	12	11	29	48	55	36
19	Rotherham County	42	8	9	4	23	21	4	3	14	14	32	37	53	36
20	Stoke	42	9	5	7	26	16	3	6	12	20	40	46	56	35
21	Coventry City	42	8	6	7	24	25	4	5	12	15	45	39	70	35
22	Stockport County	42	8	6	7	30	24	1	6	14	12	51	42	75	30

81

1921-22   6th in Division 2

Average (Home) Attendance: 11275 (based on estimates)

#	Date	Match	Result	Walker	Cresswell	Maitland	Wilson	Scott	Hutchinson	Charlton	Woods	Casson	Hawes	Richardson	Stothard	Metcalf	Robson JW	Keenlyside	Oxberry	Hetherington	Smith	Gray	Greenwell	Young	Robson G	Docherty	Mason	Ridley	Simms	Hardy	Merritt
1	Aug 27	Hull City	1-1 Casson	1	2	3	4	5	6	7	8	9	10	11																	
2	29	STOKE	1-1 Casson	1	2	3	4	5	6	7	8	9	10	11																	
3	Sep 3	HULL CITY	1-0 Hawes	1	2	3	4	5	6	7	8	9	10	11																	
4	5	Stoke	1-2 Woods	1	2	3	4			7	8	9	10	11	5	6															
5	10	Leicester City	0-1	1	2	3	4			7	8	9	10	11	5		6														
6	17	LEICESTER CITY	1-0 Richardson	1	2	3	4				8	9	10	11	5		6	7													
7	24	West Ham United	1-1 Woods	1	2	3	4			5	8	9		11			6	7	10												
8	Oct 1	WEST HAM UNITED	1-0 Keenlyside	1	2	3	4			5		8	9	11			6	7	10												
9	8	Leeds United	0-0	1	2	3	4			5		8		11			6	7	10	9											
10	15	LEEDS UNITED	0-1	1	2	3	4			5		8		11			6	7	10	9											
11	22	Port Vale	1-1 Hetherington	1	2	3	4			5		8		10	11		6	7		9											
12	29	PORT VALE	0-1	1	2	3	4			5		8		10	11		6	7		9											
13	Nov 5	Bury	0-1	1	2	3				5		9		10	11		4	6	7		8										
14	12	BURY	1-1 Greenwell	1	2	3				5		8		11			4	6		10			7	9							
15	19	BRISTOL CITY	2-0 Greenwell(2)	1	2	3				6		8		10	11		4						7	9						5	
16	26	Bristol City	1-0 Gray	1	2	3				6		8		10	11		4						7	9						5	
17	Dec 3	NOTTINGHAM FOREST	0-0	1	2	3				6		8		10			4						7	9	11					5	
18	10	Nottingham Forest	0-1	1	2	3				6		8	9	11			4						7	10						5	
19	17	WOLVERHAMPTON WANDS.	0-2	1		3				6				10			4		11			8	7	9		2				5	
20	24	Wolverhampton Wanderers	2-3 Hetherington(2)	1	2	3				6							4		11	9	8	7	10							5	
21	26	Coventry City	1-0 Keenlyside	1	2	3				6							4		11	9	8	7	10							5	
22	31	BARNSLEY	5-2 Metcalf,Gray,Smith(2),Hetherington	1	2	3				6							4		11	9	8	7	10							5	
23	Jan 2	COVENTRY CITY	2-1 Smith, Greenwell	1	2	3				6				5	4				11	9	8	7	10								
24	21	Notts County	0-2	1	2	3				6							4		11	9	8	7	10							5	
25	28	ROTHERHAM COUNTY	2-0 Smith, Hetherington	1	2	3				6							4		11	9	8	7	10							5	
26	Feb 4	Crystal Palace	2-1 Smith(2)	1	2	3				6							4		11	9	8		10		7					5	
27	11	CRYSTAL PALACE	1-1 Smith	1	2	3				6							4		11	9	8	7	10							5	
28	18	Rotherham County	1-1 Smith	1		3				6							4		11	9	8	7	10					2		5	
29	27	Barnsley	1-2 Greenwell	1		3				6							4		7	9	8		10				11	2		5	
30	Mar 4	Sheffield Wednesday	3-0 Hetherington, Keenlyside(2)	1		3				6							4		11	9	8	7	10					2		5	
31	11	SHEFFIELD WED.	0-0	1		3				6							4		11	9	8	7	10					2		5	
32	15	NOTTS COUNTY	0-0	1		3				6							4		11	10	9	8	7					2	9	5	
33	18	FULHAM	1-0 Gray	1		3				6							4		11	10	8	7						2	9	5	
34	25	Fulham	0-3	1		3				6				5	4				7	10	8						11	2	9		
35	Apr 1	BLACKPOOL	2-1 Smith, Simms	1		3				6							4		11	8	7	10		2					9	5	
36	8	Blackpool	0-4	1		3				6							4		11		8		10					2	9	5	7
37	14	DERBY COUNTY	3-1 Maitlands(pen),Simms,Hetherington	1		3				6							4		11		10	8	7					2	9	5	
38	15	BRADFORD	1-0 Simms	1		3				6							4		11		10	8	7					2	9	5	
39	17	Derby County	2-0 Hutchinson, Hetherington	1		3				6							4		11	10	9	8	7					2		5	
40	22	Bradford	0-1	1		3				6							4		11	10	9	8	7					2		5	
41	29	CLAPTON ORIENT	1-1 Keenlyside	1		3				6							4		11		10	8	7					2	9	5	
42	May 6	Clapton Orient	1-0 Smith	1		3				6					4				11	10	8	7						2	9	5	
				42	26	42	12	3	3	39	5	18	9	14	16	6	30	10	31	8	25	25	25	20	1	2	1	2	14	9	26	1
					1					1		2	2	1	1		1		5		8	10	3	5					3		

F.A. Cup

#	Date	Match	Result	Att	Walker	Cresswell	Maitland	Wilson	Scott	Hutchinson	Charlton	Woods	Casson	Hawes	Richardson	Stothard	Metcalf	Robson JW	Keenlyside	Oxberry	Hetherington	Smith	Gray	Greenwell	Young	Robson G	Docherty	Mason	Ridley	Simms	Hardy	Merritt
R1	Jan 7	Southampton	1-3 Greenwell	14497	1	2	3				6	7				4			11		9	8		10						5		

N.B. Between 21 January and 4 March, newspapers published inaccurate details of the South Shields forward line in away matches (seemingly as supplied by the club to obscure Andy Gray's absences from the North-east).

Credit is due to the Shields Football Gazette reporter, 'Wanderer', for correcting some details retrospectively.

(Docherty, was reported as 'easily the best forward' at Rotherham, yet only played one match - at Crystal Palace. Charlton, who didn't play at Sheffield Wednesday was credited with scoring two goals)

A study of several newspapers and some informed guesswork has produced the line-ups shown here which are as accurate as it has been possible to determine.

1921/22 Football League Division 2

			Home			Away					
	P	W	D	L	F	A	W	D	L	F	A	F	A	Pts
1 Nottingham Forest	42	13	7	1	29	9	9	5	7	22	21	51	30	56
2 Stoke	42	9	11	1	31	11	9	5	7	29	33	60	44	52
3 Barnsley	42	14	5	2	43	18	8	3	10	24	34	67	52	52
4 West Ham United	42	15	3	3	39	13	5	5	11	13	26	52	39	48
5 Hull City	42	13	5	3	36	13	6	5	10	15	28	51	41	48
6 SOUTH SHIELDS	42	11	7	3	25	13	6	5	10	18	25	43	38	46
7 Fulham	42	14	5	2	41	8	4	4	13	16	30	57	38	45
8 Leeds United	42	10	8	3	31	12	6	5	10	17	26	48	38	45
9 Leicester City	42	11	6	4	30	16	3	11	7	9	18	39	34	45
10 Sheffield Wed.	42	12	4	5	31	24	3	10	8	16	26	47	50	44
11 Bury	42	11	3	7	35	19	4	7	10	19	36	54	55	40
12 Derby County	42	11	3	7	34	22	4	6	11	26	42	60	64	39
13 Notts County	42	10	7	4	34	18	2	8	11	13	33	47	51	39
14 Crystal Palace	42	9	6	6	28	20	4	7	10	17	31	45	51	39
15 Clapton Orient	42	12	4	5	33	18	3	5	13	10	32	43	50	39
16 Rotherham County	42	8	9	4	17	7	6	2	13	15	36	32	43	39
17 Wolverhampton W.	42	8	7	6	28	19	5	4	12	16	30	44	49	37
18 Port Vale	42	10	5	6	28	19	4	3	14	15	38	43	57	36
19 Blackpool	42	11	1	9	33	27	4	4	13	11	30	44	57	35
20 Coventry City	42	8	5	8	31	21	4	5	12	20	39	51	60	34
21 Bradford Park Ave.	42	10	5	6	32	22	2	4	15	14	40	46	62	33
22 Bristol City	42	10	3	8	25	18	2	6	13	12	40	37	58	33

82

1922-23   13th in Division 2

Average (Home) Attendance: 8495 (based on estimates)
Lowest in Division 2

#	Date		Opponent	Score	Scorers	Walker	Ridley	Maitland	Hird	Hardy	Metcalf	Faulkner	Smith	Simms	Oxberry	Keenlyside	Wilson	McCracken	Hetherington	Hutchinson	Greenwell	Gray	Robson JW	Stothard	Robson G	Guyan	Crown	Mason	Reay	Thompson	Merritt
1	Aug	26	SOUTHAMPTON	0-0		1	2	3	4	5	6	7	8	9	10	11															
2		28	Notts County	0-2		1	2	3	4	5	6	7	8	9	10	11															
3	Sep	2	Southampton	2-0	Simms(2)	1	2	3	4	5	6	7	8	9	10	11															
4		4	NOTTS COUNTY	1-0	Simms	1	2	3	4	5	6	7	8	9	10	11															
5		9	BURY	0-2		1	2	3	4	5	6	7	8	9	10	11															
6		16	Bury	0-1		1	2	3		5	6	7	8	9		11	4	10													
7		23	ROTHERHAM COUNTY	2-0	Smith, Keenlyside	1	2	3		5	6	7	8	9		11	4		10												
8		30	Rotherham County	1-2	Hardy	1	2	3		5		7	8			11	4		9	6	10										
9	Oct	7	STOCKPORT COUNTY	3-0	Hardy(2), Greenwell	1	2	3		5	4	7	8			11			9	6	10										
10		14	Stockport County	1-1	Greenwell	1	2	3		5			8			7	4	11	9	6	10										
11		21	BRADFORD CITY	0-0		1	2	3		5			8	9		7	4	11		6	10										
12		28	Bradford City	0-1		1	2	3		5			8			7	4	11	9	6	10										
13	Nov	4	DERBY COUNTY	3-1	Smith, Wilson, Keenlyside	1	2	3	4	5			8			11	9			10	6		7								
14		11	Derby County	0-1		1	2	3	4	5			8			11	9			10	6		7								
15		18	Leeds United	1-0	Oxberry	1	2	3		5			8		10	11	4			9	6		7								
16		25	LEEDS UNITED	0-2		1	2	3		5			8		10	11	4			9			7	6							
17	Dec	2	West Ham United	0-1		1	2	3		5	6		8		10	11	9			7				4							
18		9	WEST HAM UNITED	0-0		1	2	3		5	4		8		10	11	9				6		7								
19		16	Clapton Orient	0-0		1	2	3	4	5		7		9	11		8	10			6										
20		23	CLAPTON ORIENT	3-0	Oxberry(2), Keenlyside	1	2	3	4	5				9	10	11	8				6		7								
21		25	Port Vale	0-3		1	2	3	4	5				9	10	11	8				6		7								
22		30	Wolverhampton Wanderers	0-1		1	2	3	4	5				9	10	11	8				6		7								
23	Jan	1	PORT VALE	3-1	Smith, Oxberry, Keenlyside	1	2	3	4	5			8	9	10	11					6		7								
24		6	WOLVERHAMPTON WANDS.	1-1	Gray	1	2	3	4	5			8	9	10	11					6		7								
25		20	Coventry City	2-0	Smith, Simms	1		3	4	5			8	9	10	11					6		7		2						
26		27	COVENTRY CITY	0-0		1		3	4	5			8	9	10	11	2				6		7								
27	Feb	10	Blackpool	0-3		1		3	4	5		7		9	10	11	8				6				2						
28		17	LEICESTER CITY	2-1	Smith, Oxberry	1		3		5		7	8	9	10	11	4				6				2						
29		26	Leicester City	0-3		1		3	4	5		7	8			11	10				6				2	9					
30	Mar	3	BARNSLEY	2-0	Gray, Oxberry	1		3	4	5				8	10	11					6		7				9	2			
31		10	Barnsley	0-5		1		3	4	5				8	10						6		7				9	2	11		
32		17	Sheffield Wednesday	0-2		1		3	4	5				9	10				11	6							8	2		7	
33		21	BLACKPOOL	1-0	Maitland(pen)	1	2	3	4	5				8		11					6					9				7	10
34		24	SHEFFIELD WED.	1-1	Smith(pen)	1		3	4	5			8			11					6					9	2			7	10
35		30	Manchester United	0-3		1		3	4	5			8			11			10	6					9	2			7		
36		31	Hull City	0-2		1		3	4	5			8			11			10	6					9	2			7		
37	Apr	2	MANCHESTER UNITED	0-3		1		3	4	5			7						8	6					9	2				10	11
38		7	HULL CITY	0-0		1		3	4	5		7	8		10		9			6						2	11				
39		14	Crystal Palace	1-1	Oxberry	1		3		5		7	8	9	10	11	4			6						2					
40		21	CRYSTAL PALACE	2-0	Oxberry, Keenlyside	1		3		5		7	8	9	10	11	4			6						2					
41		28	Fulham	1-0	Smith	1		3		5		7	8	9		11	4			6						2				10	
42	May	5	FULHAM	2-0	Simms, Keenlyside	1		3		5		7	8	9		11	4			6						2				10	
						42	25	42	26	42	10	18	36	22	25	38	25	5	12	33	5	13	1	1	4	9	12	2	5	5	1
													1	3			7	5	8	6	1					2	2				

F.A. Cup

	Date		Opponent	Score	Scorers	Att	Walker	Ridley	Maitland	Hird	Hardy	Metcalf	Faulkner	Smith	Simms	Oxberry	Keenlyside	Wilson	Hetherington	Greenwell	Crown
R1	Jan	13	HALIFAX TOWN	3-1	Maitland, Oxberry, Keenlyside	10734	1	2	3	4	5			8	9	10	11			6	7
R2	Feb	3	BLACKBURN ROVERS	0-0		18750	1		3	4	5		7	8	9	10	11			6	2
R2r		8	Blackburn Rovers	1-0	Smith	15358	1		3	4	5		7	8	9	10	11			6	2
R3		24	Queens Park Rangers	0-3		15099	1	2	3	4	5			8	9	10	11			6	7

1922/23 Football League Division 2

		P	W	D	L	F	A	W	D	L	F	A	F	A	Pts
1	Notts County	42	16	1	4	29	15	7	6	8	17	19	46	34	53
2	West Ham United	42	9	8	4	21	11	11	3	7	42	27	63	38	51
3	Leicester City	42	14	2	5	42	19	7	7	7	23	25	65	44	51
4	Manchester United	42	10	6	5	25	17	7	8	6	26	19	51	36	48
5	Blackpool	42	12	4	5	37	14	6	7	8	23	29	60	43	47
6	Bury	42	14	5	2	41	16	4	6	11	14	30	55	46	47
7	Leeds United	42	11	8	2	26	10	7	3	11	17	26	43	36	47
8	Sheffield Wed.	42	14	3	4	36	16	3	9	9	18	31	54	47	46
9	Barnsley	42	12	4	5	42	21	5	7	9	20	30	62	51	45
10	Fulham	42	10	7	4	29	12	6	5	10	14	20	43	32	44
11	Southampton	42	10	5	6	28	21	4	9	8	12	19	40	40	42
12	Hull City	42	9	8	4	29	22	5	6	10	14	23	43	45	42
13	SOUTH SHIELDS	42	11	7	3	26	12	4	3	14	9	32	35	44	40
14	Derby County	42	9	5	7	25	16	5	6	10	21	34	46	50	39
15	Bradford City	42	8	7	6	27	18	4	6	11	14	27	41	45	37
16	Crystal Palace	42	10	7	4	33	16	3	4	14	21	46	54	62	37
17	Port Vale	42	8	6	7	23	18	6	3	12	16	33	39	51	37
18	Coventry City	42	12	2	7	35	21	3	5	13	11	42	46	63	37
19	Clapton Orient	42	9	6	6	26	17	3	6	12	14	33	40	50	36
20	Stockport County	42	10	6	5	32	24	4	2	15	11	34	43	58	36
21	Rotherham County	42	10	7	4	30	19	3	2	16	14	44	44	63	35
22	Wolverhampton W.	42	9	4	8	32	26	0	5	16	10	51	42	77	27

83

1923-24 9th in Division 2

Average (Home) Attendance: 8855 (based on estimates)

#	Date	Opponent	Score	Scorers	Walker	Ridley	Crown	Smith	Hardy	Hutchinson	Bolam	Hetherington	Simms	Greenwell	Brown	Hird	Wilson	Stothard	Matthewson	Parker	Oxberry	Metcalf	Stannard	Guyan	Robson	Richardson	Thompson	Chape
1	Aug 25	Fulham	3-2	Hetherington(2), Simms	1	2	3	4	5	6	7	8	9	10	11													
2	27	BLACKPOOL	1-0	Bolam	1	2	3	8	5	6	7		9	10	11	4												
3	Sep 1	FULHAM	1-0	Greenwell	1	2	3		5	6	7	8	9	10	11	4												
4	3	Blackpool	1-1	Hetherington	1	2	3			6	7	8	9	10	11	4		5										
5	8	BARNSLEY	2-0	Simms, Greenwell	1	2	3			6	7	8	9	10	11	4		5										
6	15	Barnsley	0-1		1	2	3		5	6	7	8	9	10	11	4												
7	22	MANCHESTER UNITED	1-0	Simms	1	2	3		5	6	7	8	9	10	11	4												
8	29	Manchester United	1-1	Hetherington	1	2	3		5	6	7	8	9	10	11	4												
9	Oct 6	Bury	1-0	Simms	1	2	3		5	6	7	8	9	10	11	4												
10	13	BURY	1-0	Greenwell	1	2	3		5	6	7	8	9	10	11	4												
11	20	Clapton Orient	0-3		1	2	3		5	6	7	8	9	10	11	4												
12	27	CLAPTON ORIENT	1-1	Greenwell	1	2	3	8	5	6	7		9	10	11	4												
13	Nov 3	Oldham Athletic	0-1		1	2	3		5	6	11	8	9	10		4		7										
14	10	OLDHAM ATHLETIC	2-0	Simms(2)	1	2	3		5	6	7	8	9	10	11	4												
15	24	STOCKPORT COUNTY	3-1	Ridley(pen), Hardy, Simms	1	2	3		5	6	7	8	9	10		4				11								
16	Dec 1	Leicester City	1-4	Simms	1	2	3		5	6	7	8	9	10		4				11								
17	8	LEICESTER CITY	1-2	Simms	1	2	3			6	7	8	9	10		4	5			11								
18	10	Stockport County	2-3	Hetherington, Greenwell	1	2	3			6	7	9		10		4	5			11	8							
19	15	Southampton	0-0		1	2	3				7	9		10		4	5			11	8	6						
20	22	SOUTHAMPTON	1-2	Hetherington	1	2	3	8	5		7	9		10		4				11		6						
21	Jan 1	PORT VALE	3-3	Smith, Stannard, Greenwell	1	2	3	8	5		11			10		4			7				6	9				
22	5	LEEDS UNITED	2-0	Crown, Greenwell	1	2	3	8	5		11			10		4			7				6	9				
23	19	Derby County	1-6	Crown(pen)	1	2	3	8	5							4			7	11	10	6		9				
24	21	Port Vale	1-1	Parker	1		2	4	5		8								7	11	10	6		9	3			
25	26	DERBY COUNTY	3-2	Matthewson, Guyan(2)	1			8	5		11					4	2		7		10	6		9	3			
26	Feb 2	Nelson	2-0	Guyan, Oxberry	1	2		8	5		11					4			7		10	6		9	3			
27	9	NELSON	3-0	Crown(pen), Guyan, Collinson (og)	1	2	3	8	5		11					4			7		10	6		9				
28	16	Hull City	0-1			2	3	8	5		11					4			7		10	6		9	1			
29	23	HULL CITY	0-1			2		8	5		11					4			7		10	6		9	3	1		
30	27	Leeds United	1-2	Matthewson		2		8	5	6	11					4			7		10			9	3	1		
31	Mar 1	Stoke City	0-0		1		2	8	5	6	11	9				4			7		10				3			
32	8	STOKE CITY	1-0	Heatherington		2		8	5	6		9			11	4			7		10				3	1		
33	15	CRYSTAL PALACE	2-0	Hardy, Smith		2		8	5	6						4			7		10				3	1		
34	22	Crystal Palace	0-1		1		2	8	5	6	11	9				4			7		10				3			
35	29	SHEFFIELD WED.	1-1	Smith	1		2	8	5	6	11					4			7					9	3		10	
36	Apr 5	Sheffield Wednesday	0-5		1		2	8	5	6					11	4			7					9	3		10	
37	12	COVENTRY CITY	4-2	Smith(2), Guyan, Thompson	1	2	3	8	5	6					11	4			7					9			10	
38	18	BRADFORD CITY	0-0		1	2	3	8	6	5					11	4			7					9			10	
39	19	Coventry City	0-1		1	2		8		5					11	4					6			9	3		10	
40	21	Bradford City	1-0	Guyan	1	2		8		5					11				7		6			9	3		10	4
41	26	BRISTOL CITY	1-1	Brown	1	2		8		5					11	4			7		6			9	3		10	
42	May 3	Bristol City	0-1		1	2		10	5	4		8							7		6			9	3		11	
				Apps	37	32	36	26	34	31	32	23	17	22	20	17	25	3	23	8	14	15	2	16	15	5	8	1
				Goals		1	3	5	2		1	7	9	7	1				2	1	1		1	6			1	

1 own goal

F.A. Cup

#	Date	Opponent	Score	Scorers	Att	Walker	Ridley	Crown	Smith	Hardy	Bolam	Brown	Wilson	Matthewson	Guyan	Robson
R1	Jan 12	Burnley	2-3	Hetherington, Parker	20600	1	2	3	8	5	11	10	4	7	6	9

1923/24 Football League Division 2

		P	Home W	Home D	Home L	Home F	Home A	Away W	Away D	Away L	Away F	Away A	F	A	Pts
1	Leeds United	42	14	5	2	41	10	7	7	7	20	25	61	35	54
2	Bury	42	15	5	1	42	7	6	4	11	21	28	63	35	51
3	Derby County	42	15	4	2	52	15	6	5	10	23	27	75	42	51
4	Blackpool	42	13	7	1	43	12	5	6	10	29	35	72	47	49
5	Southampton	42	13	5	3	36	9	4	9	8	16	22	52	31	48
6	Stoke	42	9	11	1	27	10	5	7	9	17	32	44	42	46
7	Oldham Athletic	42	10	10	1	24	12	4	7	10	21	40	45	52	45
8	Sheffield Wed.	42	15	5	1	42	9	1	7	13	12	42	54	51	44
9	SOUTH SHIELDS	42	13	5	3	34	16	4	5	12	15	34	49	50	44
10	Clapton Orient	42	11	7	3	27	10	3	8	10	13	26	40	36	43
11	Barnsley	42	12	7	2	34	16	4	4	13	23	45	57	61	43
12	Leicester City	42	13	4	4	43	16	4	4	13	21	38	64	54	42
13	Stockport County	42	10	7	4	32	21	3	9	9	12	31	44	52	42
14	Manchester United	42	10	7	4	37	15	3	7	11	15	29	52	44	40
15	Crystal Palace	42	11	7	3	37	19	2	6	13	16	46	53	65	39
16	Port Vale	42	9	5	7	33	29	4	7	10	17	37	50	66	38
17	Hull City	42	8	7	6	32	23	2	10	9	14	28	46	51	37
18	Bradford City	42	8	7	6	24	21	3	8	10	11	27	35	48	37
19	Coventry City	42	9	6	6	34	23	2	7	12	18	45	52	68	35
20	Fulham	42	9	8	4	30	20	1	6	14	15	36	45	56	34
21	Nelson	42	8	8	5	32	31	2	5	14	8	43	40	74	33
22	Bristol City	42	5	8	8	19	26	2	7	12	13	39	32	65	29

1924-25 9th in Division 2

Average (Home) Attendance: 9035 (based on estimates)

Player columns (left to right): Walker, Ridley, Crown, Wilson, Hutchinson, Metcalf, Matthewson, Smith, Harris, Greenwell, Trotter, Oxberry, Hird, Devan, Guyan, Pattison, Hunter, Thompson, Gascoigne, Richardson, Grenyer, Robson

#	Date	Opponent	Score	Scorers	Wa	Ri	Cr	Wi	Hu	Me	Ma	Sm	Ha	Gr	Tr	Ox	Hi	De	Gu	Pa	Hun	Th	Ga	Rich	Gre	Ro
1	Aug 30	PORTSMOUTH	0-2		1	2	3	4	5	6	7	8	9	10	11											
2	Sep 1	BLACKPOOL	1-3	Oxberry	1	2	3	4	5	6	7	8	9		11	10										
3	Sep 6	Fulham	1-1	Guyan	1	2	3	4	5					10	11	8	6	7	9							
4	Sep 8	Blackpool	0-5		1	2	3	4	5					10	11	8	6	7	9							
5	Sep 13	WOLVERHAMPTON WANDS.	3-3	Oxberry, Trotter(2)	1	2				6	4	7		10	9	8		11			3	5				
6	Sep 20	Barnsley	0-1		1	2				6	4	7		9		8		11			3	5	10			
7	Sep 27	MIDDLESBROUGH	0-1		1	2	3			6	4	7		9		8		11				5	10			
8	Oct 4	Port Vale	0-0		1	2	3			6	4	7			11	8	10	9				5				
9	Oct 11	BRADFORD CITY	1-0	Oxberry	1	2	3			6	4	7		10		8		11	9			5				
10	Oct 18	Oldham Athletic	0-1		1	2	3			6	4	7		10		8		11	9			5				
11	Oct 25	SHEFFIELD WED.	0-1		1	2	3	9	6	4			8		11	10		7				5				
12	Nov 1	Clapton Orient	0-0		1	2	3			6	4	7	8	10		9		11				5				
13	Nov 8	CRYSTAL PALACE	1-1	Oxberry	1	2	3			6	4	7	8	10		9		11					5			
14	Nov 15	Southampton	1-1	Smith		2			6	4	7	8			11	9					5	10		1		3
15	Nov 22	CHELSEA	1-1	Matthewson		2			6	4	7	8			11	9					5	10		1		3
16	Nov 29	Stockport County	0-0			2			6	4	7	8			11	9					5	10		1		3
17	Dec 6	MANCHESTER UNITED	1-2	Oxberry		2			6	4	7	8			11	9					5	10		1		3
18	Dec 13	Leicester City	1-1	Smith		2			6	4	7	8			11	9					5	10		1		3
19	Dec 20	STOKE CITY	4-0	Matthewson, Smith, Thompson(2)		2		4	6		7	8			11	9					5	10		1		3
20	Dec 25	Coventry City	1-0	Oxberry		2		4	6		7	8			11	9					5	10		1		3
21	Dec 27	Portsmouth	0-2			2		4	6		7	8			11	9					5	10		1		3
22	Jan 1	COVENTRY CITY	4-1	Ridley(pen), Matthewson, Smith, Oxberry		2		4	6		7	8			11	9						10	5	1		3
23	Jan 17	Wolverhampton Wanderers	1-2	Matthewson		2		4	6		7	8				9		11			5	10		1		3
24	Jan 24	BARNSLEY	5-2	Ridley(pen), Hunter, Matthewson(2), Trotter		2		4	6		7	8			11	9					5	10		1		3
25	Jan 31	Middlesbrough	1-1	Matthewson		2		4	6		7	8			11	9					5	10		1		3
26	Feb 7	PORT VALE	3-0	Smith, Oxberry(2)		2		4	6		7	8			11	9					5	10		1		3
27	Feb 14	Bradford City	0-1			2		4	6		7	8			11	9					5	10		1		3
28	Feb 21	OLDHAM ATHLETIC	0-0			2			5	6	7	8			11	9		4				10		1		3
29	Feb 25	FULHAM	2-1	Thompson, Trotter		2		4		6	7	8			11	9						10	5	1		3
30	Feb 28	Sheffield Wednesday	1-0	Smith		2			5	6	4	7	8		11	9						10		1		3
31	Mar 7	CLAPTON ORIENT	2-0	Oxberry(2)		2			5	6	4	7	8		11	9						10		1		3
32	Mar 14	Crystal Palace	0-0			2			5	6	4	7	8		11	9						10		1		3
33	Mar 21	SOUTHAMPTON	1-1	Oxberry		2			5	6	4	7	8		11	9						10		1		3
34	Apr 1	HULL CITY	2-0	Smith, Oxberry		2			5	6	4	7	8		11	9						10		1		3
35	Apr 4	Stockport County	0-1			2			5	6	4	7	8		11	9						10		1		3
36	Apr 10	DERBY COUNTY	1-0	Thompson		2			5	6	4	7	8		11	9						10		1		3
37	Apr 11	Manchester United	0-1			2			5	6	4	7	8		11	9						10		1		3
38	Apr 13	Derby County	0-0			2				6	4	7	8		11	9		5				10		1		3
39	Apr 18	LEICESTER CITY	1-1	Oxberry		2			5	6	4	7	8		11	9						10		1		3
40	Apr 20	Chelsea	1-1	Thompson		2			8	6	4	7			11	9		5				10		1		3
41	Apr 25	Stoke City	0-0			2			8	6	4	7			11				9			10		1		3
42	May 2	Hull City	1-0	Thompson		2			8		4	7			11	9		9	5			10		1	6	3
		Appearances			13	42	11	27	40	31	39	31	2	5	41	39	7	12	6	2	21	31	3	29	1	29
		Goals				2					7	7			4	14					1	6				

F.A. Cup

R	Date	Opponent	Score	Scorers	Wa	Ri	Cr	Wi	Hu	Me	Ma	Sm	Ha	Gr	Tr	Ox	Hi	De	Gu	Pa	Hun	Th	Ga	Rich	Gre	Ro
R1	Jan 10	Crystal Palace	1-2	Thompson		2			4	6		7	8		11	9					5	10		1		3

1924/25 Football League Division 2

				Home				Away						
		P	W	D	L	F	A	W	D	L	F	A	F	A	Pts
1	Leicester City	42	15	4	2	58	9	9	7	5	32	23	90	32	59
2	Manchester United	42	17	3	1	40	6	6	8	7	17	17	57	23	57
3	Derby County	42	15	3	3	49	15	7	8	6	22	21	71	36	55
4	Portsmouth	42	7	13	1	28	14	8	5	8	30	36	58	50	48
5	Chelsea	42	11	8	2	31	12	5	7	9	20	25	51	37	47
6	Wolverhampton W.	42	14	1	6	29	19	6	5	10	26	32	55	51	46
7	Southampton	42	12	8	1	29	10	1	10	10	11	26	40	36	44
8	Port Vale	42	12	4	5	34	19	5	4	12	14	37	48	56	42
9	SOUTH SHIELDS	42	9	6	6	33	21	3	11	7	9	17	42	38	41
10	Hull City	42	12	6	3	40	14	3	5	13	10	35	50	49	41
11	Clapton Orient	42	8	7	6	22	13	6	5	10	20	29	42	42	40
12	Fulham	42	11	6	4	26	15	4	4	13	15	41	41	56	40
13	Middlesbrough	42	6	10	5	22	21	4	9	8	14	23	36	44	39
14	Sheffield Wed.	42	12	3	6	36	23	3	5	13	14	33	50	56	38
15	Barnsley	42	8	8	5	30	23	5	4	12	16	36	46	59	38
16	Bradford City	42	11	6	4	26	13	2	6	13	11	37	37	50	38
17	Blackpool	42	8	5	8	37	26	6	4	11	28	35	65	61	37
18	Oldham Athletic	42	9	5	7	24	21	4	6	11	11	30	35	51	37
19	Stockport County	42	10	6	5	26	15	3	5	13	11	42	37	57	37
20	Stoke	42	7	8	6	22	17	5	3	13	12	29	34	46	35
21	Crystal Palace	42	8	4	9	23	19	4	6	11	15	35	38	54	34
22	Coventry City	42	10	6	5	32	26	1	3	17	13	58	45	84	31

1925-26 9th in Division 2

Average (Home) Attendance: 7325 (Lowest in Division 2)

Official Attendances available from 1925-26 season.

#	Date	Opponent	Score	Scorers	Att.	Pearson	Ridley	Robson	Metcalf	Hunter	Hutchinson	Matthewson	Wilson	Oxberry	Smith JW	Trotter	Crown	Guyan	Greenwell	Thirlaway	Richardson	Parker	Hird	Atkinson	Henderson
1	Aug 29	Swansea Town	2-1	Oxberry(2)	20505	1	2	3	4	5	6	7	8	9	10	11									
2	Sep 5	SHEFFIELD WED.	1-1	Wilson	10312	1	2	3	4	5	6	7	8	9	10	11									
3	7	WOLVERHAMPTON WANDS.	3-1	Smith, Guyan(2)	6787	1	2		4	5	6	7		9	10		8	11	3						
4	12	Stoke City	1-0	Matthewson	11455	1	2		4	5	6	7		9	10		8	11	3						
5	14	Wolverhampton Wanderers	0-2		15687	1	2		4	5	6	7		9	10		8	11	3						
6	19	OLDHAM ATHLETIC	0-0		8647	1	2		4	5	6	7		9	10		8	11	3						
7	26	Stockport County	1-4	Smith	5239	1	2		4	5	6	7		9	10		8	11	3						
8	Oct 3	FULHAM	5-2	Hutchinson, Matthewson, Smith, Wilson, Trotter	7321	1	2		4	5	6	7		9	10		8	11	3	10					
9	10	Hull City	3-1	Hutchinson, Wilson(2)	10092	1	2		4	5	6		9	8	10		11	3		10	7				
10	17	CHELSEA	0-0		11805	1	2		4	5	6		9	8	10		11	3		10	7				
11	24	Clapton Orient	2-1	Wilson(2)	13784	1	2		4	5	6		9	8	10		11	3		10	7				
12	26	PORTSMOUTH	5-1	Smith, Wilson, Greenwell, Trotter, Watson(og)	4569	1	2		4	5	6		9	8	10		11	3		10	7				
13	31	BLACKPOOL	3-4	Thirlaway, JW Smith, Trotter	10178	1	2		4	5	6		9	8	10		11	3		10	7				
14	Nov 7	Darlington	1-4	Smith	6449	1	2		4	5	6		9	8	10		11	3		10	7				
15	14	BRADFORD CITY	1-3	Thirlaway	6901	1	2		4	5	6		9	8	10		11	3		10	7				
16	21	Derby County	0-2		13822		2		4	5	6			10	8	11	3			7	1	9			
17	28	NOTTINGHAM FOREST	3-1	Wilson(2), Trotter	4293		2		4	5	6			10	8	11	3			7	1	9			
18	Dec 5	Southampton	1-0	Wilson	9848		2		4	5	6			10	8	11	3			7	1	9			
19	7	Portsmouth	2-4	Smith, Parker	5918		2		4	5	6			10	8	11	3			7	1	9			
20	12	BARNSLEY	3-0	Thirlaway, Wilson, Parker	6167		2		4	5	6			10	8	11	3			7	1	9			
21	19	Port Vale	0-2		8794		2		4	5	6			10	8	11	3			7	1	9			
22	26	Preston North End	4-0	Thirlaway, Smith, Parker(2)	29886		2		4	5	6			10	8	11	3			7	1	9			
23	Jan 1	Middlesbrough	2-1	Parker(2)	19007		2		4	5	6			10	8	11	3			7	1	9			
24	2	SWANSEA TOWN	3-1	Smith, Parker, Trotter	9319		2		4	5	6			10	8	11	3			7	1	9			
25	16	Sheffield Wednesday	0-1		19555		2		4	5	6			10	8	11	3			7	1	9			
26	23	STOKE CITY	5-1	Smith(2), Parker, Wilson(2)	7114		2		4	5	6			10	8	11	3			7	1	9			
27	Feb 6	STOCKPORT COUNTY	4-2	Smith(2), Parker, Wilson	6955		2	3	4	5	6			10	8	11				7	1	9			
28	13	Fulham	1-2	Smith(pen)	22330		2		4	5	6			10	8	11	3			7	1	9			
29	27	Chelsea	0-0		38242		2		4	5	6			10	8	11	3			7	1	9			
30	Mar 3	HULL CITY	1-3	Trotter	4831		2		4	5	6			10	8	11	3			7	1	9			
31	6	SOUTHAMPTON	2-0	Hutchinson, Wilson	5776		2	3	4	5	6			10	8	11				7	1	9			
32	13	Blackpool	0-1		7640		2	3	4	5	6			10	8	11				7	1	9			
33	16	Oldham Athletic	1-2	Smith	5069		2	3	4	5	6				10	8				7	1	9			
34	20	DARLINGTON	2-4	Parker(2)	7476		2	3	4	5				10	8					7	1	9	6		
35	24	CLAPTON ORIENT	1-0	Smith	2797		2		6	5				10	8	11				7	1	9	4	3	
36	27	Bradford City	1-1	Smith	13324		2		6	5				10	8	11				7	1	9	4	3	
37	Apr 2	MIDDLESBROUGH	2-2	Hunter, Smith	14839		2	3	6	5				10	8	11				7	1	9	4		
38	3	DERBY COUNTY	0-0		7996	1	2		6	5		7	3		8	11		9				10	4		
39	5	PRESTON NORTH END	1-1	Guyan	6708	1	2		6	5		7	3		8	11		9				10	4		
40	10	Nottingham Forest	1-4	Guyan	8156	1	2		6	5		7	3		8	11		9					4		10
41	24	Barnsley	1-3	Oxberry	4901	1	2		4	5	6	7	3	10	8	11						9			
42	May 1	PORT VALE	5-2	Matthewson, Smith(2), Parker, Trotter	3027	1	2		4	5	6	7	3	10	8	11						9			
						20	42	8	42	35	13	41	5	42	42	27	9	8	29	22	25	7	2	1	
					Goals		1		3	3	15	3	20	7					4	1	4	12			

1 Own Goal

F.A. Cup

Rd	Date	Opponent	Score	Scorers	Att.	Ridley	Metcalf	Hunter	Hutchinson	Smith JW	Trotter	Thirlaway	Richardson	Parker
R3	Jan 9	CHILTON Colliery	3-0	Parker, Wilson, Trotter	14866	2	4	5	6	10	8 11 3	7	1	9
R4	30	BIRMINGHAM	2-1	Smith, Trotter	17000	2	4	5	6	10	8 11 3	7	1	9
R5	Feb 20	Bolton Wanderers	0-3		48166	2	4	5	6	10	8 11 3	7	1	9

1925/26 Football League Division 2

		P		Home				Away					F	A	Pts
			W	D	L	F	A	W	D	L	F	A			
1	Sheffield Wed.	42	19	0	2	61	17	8	6	7	27	31	88	48	60
2	Derby County	42	17	2	2	57	17	8	5	8	20	25	77	42	57
3	Chelsea	42	10	7	4	42	22	9	7	5	34	27	76	49	52
4	Wolverhampton W.	42	15	4	2	55	15	6	3	12	29	45	84	60	49
5	Swansea Town	42	13	6	2	50	16	6	5	10	27	41	77	57	49
6	Blackpool	42	12	6	3	41	16	5	5	11	35	53	76	69	45
7	Oldham Athletic	42	14	4	3	52	24	4	4	13	22	38	74	62	44
8	Port Vale	42	15	3	3	53	18	4	3	14	26	51	79	69	44
9	SOUTH SHIELDS	42	11	6	4	50	29	7	2	12	24	36	74	65	44
10	Middlesbrough	42	14	1	6	56	28	7	1	13	21	40	77	68	44
11	Portsmouth	42	12	4	5	48	27	5	6	10	31	47	79	74	44
12	Preston North End	42	17	2	2	54	28	1	5	15	17	56	71	84	43
13	Hull City	42	11	4	6	40	19	5	5	11	23	42	63	61	41
14	Southampton	42	11	2	8	39	25	4	6	11	24	38	63	63	38
15	Darlington	42	9	5	7	51	31	5	5	11	21	46	72	77	38
16	Bradford City	42	9	5	7	28	26	4	5	12	19	40	47	66	36
17	Nottingham Forest	42	11	4	6	38	25	3	4	14	13	48	51	73	36
18	Barnsley	42	10	7	4	38	22	2	5	14	20	62	58	84	36
19	Fulham	42	8	6	7	32	29	3	6	12	14	48	46	77	34
20	Clapton Orient	42	8	6	7	30	21	4	3	14	20	44	50	65	33
21	Stoke City	42	8	5	8	32	23	4	3	14	22	54	54	77	32
22	Stockport County	42	8	7	6	34	28	0	2	19	17	69	51	97	25

1926-27 — 19th in Division 2

Average (Home) Attendance: 5361 (Lowest in Division 2)

#	Date	Opponent	Score	Scorers	Att	McKenna	Ridley	Phizacklea	Metcalf	Hunter	Hutchinson	Matthewson	Smith J	Parker	Wilson	Trotter	Oxberry	Grenyer	Hird	Pattison	Loftus	Taylor	Stevenson	Scott	Dunn	Wilkinson	Smith W
1	Aug 28	NOTTS COUNTY	5-0	Matthewson(2), Smith(3)	6835	1	2	3	4	5	6	7	8	9	10	11											
2	30	Hull City	0-2		7002	1	2	3	4	5	6	7	8	9	10	11											
3	Sep 4	Clapton Orient	0-1		19745	1	2	3	4	5	6	7	8	9	10	11											
4	11	MIDDLESBROUGH	0-0		7519	1	2	3	4	5	6	7	8	9	10	11											
5	18	Port Vale	2-4	Matthewson, Parker	12474	1	2	3	4	5	6	7	8	9		11	10										
6	25	SOUTHAMPTON	1-2	Matthewson	5102	1	2	3	4	5	6	7	8	9		11	10										
7	Oct 2	Bradford City	1-3	Oxberry	12651	1	2	3	4	5		7	8	9		11	10	6									
8	9	CHELSEA	5-1	Ridley(pen),Metcalf,Matthewson(2),Oxberry	3705	1	2	3	4			7	8	9		11	10	6	5								
9	16	Fulham	2-2	Matthewson, Parker	19504	1	2	3	4			7	8	9		11	10	6	5								
10	23	GRIMSBY TOWN	3-2	Smith, Parker(2)	4871	1	2	3	4			7	8	9		11	10	6	5								
11	30	Reading	1-2	Parker	14059	1	2	3	4			7	8	9		11	10	6	5								
12	Nov 6	SWANSEA TOWN	0-1		4422	1	2	3	4			7	8	9		11	10		5								
13	13	Nottingham Forest	2-4	Matthewson, Smith	8054	1	2	3	4			7	8	10	6	11	9		5								
14	20	BARNSLEY	7-1	Matthewson(2),Parker(3),Smith,Trotter	3754	1	2	3	4			7	8	10	6	11	9		5								
15	27	Manchester City	2-1	Matthewson, Trotter	20837	1	2	3	4	5		7	8	10	6	11	9										
16	Dec 4	DARLINGTON	1-0	Trotter	5914	1	2	3	4	5		7	8	10	6	11	9										
17	11	Portsmouth	1-1	Parker	15103	1	2	3	4	5		7	8	10	6	11	9										
18	18	OLDHAM ATHLETIC	4-1	Smith(2), Oxberry, Parker	4856	1	2	3	4	5		7	8	10	6	11	9										
19	25	PRESTON NORTH END	1-1	Parker	9238	1	2	3	4	5		7	8	10	6	11	9										
20	27	Preston North End	0-4		30614	1	2	3	4	5		7	8	9	6	11	10										
21	Jan 1	HULL CITY	3-1	Matthewson, Hird, Trotter	9549	1		3	4	5	6	7	8	2		11	10		9								
22	15	Notts County	1-4	Hird	8717	1		3	4	5	6	7	8	2		11	10		9								
23	22	CLAPTON ORIENT	2-1	Matthewson, Oxberry	5676			3	4	5	6	7	8	2		11	9					10	1				
24	Feb 5	PORT VALE	3-3	Oxberry(2), Stevenson	4603			3	4	5		7	8	2		11	9	6			2	1	10				
25	12	Southampton	2-6	Smith, Stevenson	7412			3	4	5		7	8	2		11	9	6				1	10				
26	26	Chelsea	1-4	Smith	31191		2	3	4	5		7	8	9	6	11						1	10				
27	Mar 2	BRADFORD CITY	3-3	Smith, Parker(2)	2976		2	3	4	5		7	8	9			6					1	10			11	
28	5	FULHAM	1-1	Smith(pen)	4296	1		3	4	5		7	8	9	2		6						10			11	
29	12	Grimsby Town	1-1	Parker	15190		2	3	4	5		7	8	9	6	11						1	10				
30	16	Middlesbrough	0-5		25322			3	4	5		7	8	9	2	11	6					1	10				
31	19	READING	3-0	Grenyer(2), Oxberry	5333			3	4			7	8	9		11	10	6	5	2		1					
32	26	Swansea Town	0-2		9380			3	4			7	8	9	2	11	10	6	5			1					
33	Apr 2	NOTTINGHAM FOREST	1-1	Oxberry	5458			3	4			7	8	9	2	6	10	5				1		11			
34	9	Barnsley	1-6	Oxberry	2290			3	4			7		9	2	6	8	5		10	1			11			
35	15	Blackpool	1-6	Oxberry	15460	1		3	4			7	10	5		11	9	6		2							8
36	16	MANCHESTER CITY	2-2	Parker, Trotter	6543	1		3	4			7	8	9	5	11	10	6		2		1					
37	18	BLACKPOOL	2-2	Smith, Oxberry	5282			3	4			7	8	9	5	11	10	6		2		1					
38	23	Darlington	2-8	Grenyer, Oxberry	6780			3	4			7	8	9	5	10	9	6		2		1		11			
39	25	Wolverhampton Wanderers	0-2		4618			3	4			7	8	9	2		10	6				1	5	11			
40	30	PORTSMOUTH	1-0	Smith	4450		2		4			7	8	10	3	11	9	6				1	5				
41	May 2	WOLVERHAMPTON WANDS.	1-2	Grenyer	2191		2		4			7	8		9	11		6				1	5	3			10
42	7	Oldham Athletic	2-3	Smith, Stevenson	5979		2		4			7	8		5		6					1	9	11	3		10
				Apps		26	26	39	42	24	8	42	41	32	34	37	35	19	12	7	2	16	8	5	2	2	3
				Goals			1		1			12	15	16		5	12	4	2				3				

F.A. Cup

Rd	Date	Opponent	Score	Scorers	Att	McKenna	Ridley	Phizacklea	Metcalf	Hunter	Hutchinson	Matthewson	Smith J	Parker	Wilson	Trotter	Oxberry	Grenyer	Hird	Pattison	Loftus	Taylor	Stevenson	Scott	Dunn	Wilkinson	Smith W
R3	Jan 8	PLYMOUTH ARGYLE	3-1	Hunter, Smith, Oxberry	9811	1		3	4	5	6	7	8	9	2	11	10										
R4	29	Sheffield Wednesday	1-1	Matthewson	33471			3	4	5	6	7	8	2		11	9					1	10				
R4r	Feb 2	SHEFFIELD WEDNESDAY	1-0	Smith	23266			3	4	5		7	8	2		11	9	6				1	10				
R5	20	SWANSEA TOWN	2-2	Smith, Trotter	24348			3	4	5		7	8	2		11	9	6				1	10				
R5r	24	Swansea Town	1-2	Parker	24000		2	3	4	5		7	8	9	6	11						1					

1926/27 Football League Division 2

		P	W	D	L	F	A	W	D	L	F	A	F	A	Pts
				Home						Away					
1	Middlesbrough	42	18	2	1	78	23	9	6	6	44	37	122	60	62
2	Portsmouth	42	14	4	3	58	17	9	4	8	29	32	87	49	54
3	Manchester City	42	15	3	3	65	23	7	7	7	43	38	108	61	54
4	Chelsea	42	13	7	1	40	17	7	5	9	22	35	62	52	52
5	Nottingham Forest	42	14	6	1	57	23	4	8	9	23	32	80	55	50
6	Preston North End	42	14	4	3	54	29	6	5	10	20	43	74	72	49
7	Hull City	42	13	4	4	43	19	7	3	11	20	33	63	52	47
8	Port Vale	42	11	6	4	50	26	5	7	9	38	52	88	78	45
9	Blackpool	42	13	5	3	65	26	5	3	13	30	54	95	80	44
10	Oldham Athletic	42	12	3	6	50	37	7	3	11	24	47	74	84	44
11	Barnsley	42	13	5	3	56	23	4	4	13	32	64	88	87	43
12	Swansea Town	42	13	5	3	44	21	3	6	12	24	51	68	72	43
13	Southampton	42	9	8	4	35	22	6	4	11	25	40	60	62	42
14	Reading	42	14	1	6	47	20	2	7	12	17	52	64	72	40
15	Wolverhampton W.	42	10	4	7	54	30	4	3	14	19	45	73	75	35
16	Notts County	42	11	4	6	45	24	4	1	16	25	72	70	96	35
17	Grimsby Town	42	6	7	8	39	39	5	5	11	35	52	74	91	34
18	Fulham	42	11	4	6	39	31	2	4	15	19	61	58	92	34
19	SOUTH SHIELDS	42	10	8	3	49	25	1	3	17	22	71	71	96	33
20	Clapton Orient	42	9	9	3	37	35	3	4	14	23	61	60	96	31
21	Darlington	42	10	3	8	53	42	2	3	16	26	56	79	98	30
22	Bradford City	42	6	4	11	30	28	1	5	15	20	60	50	88	23

1927-28 22nd (bottom) in Division 2

Average (Home) Attendance: 5379 (Lowest in Division 2)

Player columns (left to right): Shevlin, Wilson, Phizacklea, Hutchinson, Stevenson, Davies, Matthewson, Smith JW, Ramage, Oxberry, Scott, Atkinson, Grenyer, Gibson, Smith WH, Hampson, Loftus, Turnbull, Henderson, Hardy, Parker, Wilkinson, Taylor, Hunter, Dunn, Conaty, Neilson, Cook, Maycock

#	Date	Opponent	Score	Scorers	Att.
1	Aug 27	LEEDS UNITED	1-5	Ramage	9826
2	Sep 3	Nottingham Forest	2-7	Oxberry, Scott	16714
3	5	Wolverhampton W.	1-2	JW Smith	10971
4	10	MANCHESTER CITY	0-1		7623
5	12	WOLVERHAMPTON W.	2-2	JW Smith, Oxberry	4873
6	17	Hull City	0-1		10252
7	24	PRESTON NORTH END	2-3	Oxberry, Loftus	6338
8	Oct 1	Swansea Town	3-6	Oxberry(3)	3697
9	8	FULHAM	2-1	Matthewson, JW Smith	6253
10	15	Barnsley	0-0		10611
11	22	Oldham Athletic	2-2	Oxberry(2)	10723
12	29	NOTTS COUNTY	2-3	Oxberry(2)	6379
13	Nov 5	Southampton	5-3	Henderson, JW Smith, Oxberry(2), Scott	9787
14	12	GRIMSBY TOWN	1-2	Stevenson	6430
15	19	Reading	1-5	Oxberry	6141
16	26	CLAPTON ORIENT	2-2	Loftus, Oxberry	5771
17	Dec 3	Chelsea	0-6		28719
18	10	BLACKPOOL	2-2	Oxberry, Parker	5130
19	17	West Bromwich Albion	0-3		11711
20	24	BRISTOL CITY	1-3	JW Smith	4232
21	27	Stoke City	1-3	JW Smith	13990
22	31	Leeds United	0-3		12752
23	Jan 2	STOKE CITY	2-3	Wilson, Oxberry	6480
24	7	NOTTINGHAM FOREST	3-4	Stevenson, Oxberry, Loftus	4723
25	21	Manchester City	0-3		29200
26	Feb 4	Preston North End	2-7	Oxberry, Scott	10507
27	11	SWANSEA TOWN	3-1	Oxberry(3)	3572
28	18	Fulham	0-2		15626
29	22	HULL CITY	1-0	Cook	4322
30	25	BARNSLEY	0-0		5513
31	Mar 3	OLDHAM ATHLETIC	0-3		6186
32	10	Notts County	1-4	Stevenson	8117
33	17	SOUTHAMPTON	2-1	Parker, Loftus	2650
34	24	Grimsby Town	1-4	Stevenson	7868
35	31	READING	0-0		3301
36	Apr 6	Port Vale	3-2	Maycock, Loftus(2)	11081
37	7	Clapton Orient	2-2	Wilson, Matthewson	11019
38	9	PORT VALE	0-1		4444
39	14	CHELSEA	2-1	Grenyer, Matthewson	3395
40	21	Blackpool	1-4	Maycock	8539
41	28	WEST BROMWICH A.	2-3	Stevenson, Scott	5514
42	May 5	Bristol City	1-1	Stevenson	5607

Additional Player: Brown 34/4

Appearance totals (per player column order above):
27 | 36 | 29 | 4 | 21 | 27 | 37 | 19 | 3 | 39 | 34 | 1 | 18 | 4 | 22 | 25 | 25 | 1 | 13 | 11 | 17 | 3 | 15 | 18 | 3 | 3 | 4 | 4 | 8

Goals totals:
Wilson 2, Stevenson 6, Matthewson 3, Smith JW 6, Ramage 1, Oxberry 21, Scott 4, Grenyer 1, Loftus 6, Henderson 1, Parker 2, Cook 1, Maycock 2

F.A. Cup

Round	Date	Opponent	Score	Att.
R3	Jan 14	Middlesbrough	0-3	25682

1927/28 Football League Division 2

		P	W	D	L	F	A	W	D	L	F	A	F	A	Pts
				Home					Away						
1	Manchester City	42	18	2	1	70	27	7	7	7	30	32	100	59	59
2	Leeds United	42	16	2	3	63	15	9	5	7	35	34	98	49	57
3	Chelsea	42	15	2	4	46	15	8	6	7	29	30	75	45	54
4	Preston North End	42	15	3	3	62	24	7	6	8	38	42	100	66	53
5	Stoke City	42	14	5	2	44	17	8	3	10	34	42	78	59	52
6	Swansea Town	42	13	6	2	46	17	5	6	10	29	46	75	63	48
7	Oldham Athletic	42	15	3	3	55	18	4	5	12	20	33	75	51	46
8	West Bromwich Alb.	42	17	4	0	50	28	7	5	9	40	42	90	70	46
9	Port Vale	42	11	6	4	45	20	7	2	12	23	37	68	57	44
10	Nottingham Forest	42	10	6	5	54	37	5	4	12	29	47	83	84	40
11	Grimsby Town	42	8	6	7	41	41	6	6	9	28	42	69	83	40
12	Bristol City	42	11	5	5	42	18	4	4	13	34	61	76	79	39
13	Barnsley	42	10	5	6	43	36	4	6	11	22	49	65	85	39
14	Hull City	42	9	8	4	25	19	3	7	11	16	35	41	54	39
15	Notts County	42	10	4	7	47	26	3	8	10	21	48	68	74	38
16	Wolverhampton W.	42	11	5	5	43	31	2	5	14	20	60	63	91	36
17	Southampton	42	11	3	7	54	40	3	4	14	14	37	68	77	35
18	Reading	42	9	8	4	32	22	2	5	14	21	53	53	75	35
19	Blackpool	42	11	3	7	55	43	2	5	14	28	58	83	101	34
20	Clapton Orient	42	9	7	5	32	25	2	5	14	23	60	55	85	34
21	Fulham	42	12	7	2	46	22	1	0	20	22	67	68	89	33
22	SOUTH SHIELDS	42	5	5	11	30	41	2	4	15	26	70	56	111	23

1928-29 10th in Division 3 (N)

Average (Home) Attendance: 4710

#		Date	Opponent	Score	Scorers	Att	Shevlin	Sinclair	Dunn	Hope	Davies	Reilly	Matthewson	Stevenson	Kennedy	Parker	Scott G	Grenyer	Scott John	Loftus	Maycock	Talbot JH	Turnbull	Cook	Scott Joseph	Littlewood	Taylor	Creighton
1	Aug	25	Darlington	2-2	Matthewson, Stevenson	7253	1	2	3	4	5	6	7	8	9	10	11											
2	Sep	1	SOUTHPORT	4-0	Stevenson,Kennedy,Parker,G Scott	6215	1	2	3	4	5	6	7	8	9	10	11											
3		8	Rochdale	2-1	Parker(2)	6913	1	2	3	4	5		7	8	9	10	11	6										
4		12	Nelson	0-1		5843	1	2	3	4	5		7	8	9	10	11	6										
5		15	NEW BRIGHTON	0-2		5533	1	2	3	4	5		7	8	9	10	11	6										
6		22	Wrexham	0-1		10148	1	2	3	4	5		7		9	10	11		6	8								
7		29	CHESTERFIELD	6-3	Hope,Matthewson(2),Maycock(2),Parker	4696	1	2	3	4	5	6	7			10	11			8	9							
8	Oct	6	Barow	1-1	Kennedy	6584	1	2	3	4	5	6	7		8						9	11						
9		13	DONCASTER ROVERS	1-0	Reilly	4913	1	2	3	4	5	6	7		8	10	11				9							
10		20	Hartlepools United	5-0	Matthewson,Stevenson,Maycock,Parker(2)	5130	1	2	3	4	5	6	7	8		10	11				9							
11		27	CARLISLE UNITED	5-0	Coulthard(og),Matthewson,Stevenson,Maycock,Parker	9157	1	2	3	4	5	6	7	8		10					9	11						
12	Nov	3	Rotherham United	1-1	Stevenson	5167	1	2	3	4	5	6	7	8		10					9	11						
13		10	WIGAN BOROUGH	2-2	Stevenson, Maycock	5450	1	2		4	5	6	7	8		10					9	11	3					
14		17	Crewe Alexandra	5-1	Matthewson,Stevenson,Maycock(2),Parker	4233	1	2		4	5	6	7	8		10					9	11						
15	Dec	1	Stockport County	1-7	Maycock	10690	1	2		4	5	6	7	8		10					9	11						
16		8	HALIFAX TOWN	2-1	Reilly, Matthewson	4172	1	2		4	5	6	7	8		10					9	11						
17		15	Lincoln City	0-5		5337	1	2		4	5	6	7	8		10					9	11						
18		22	BRADFORD CITY	1-1	Matthewson	4297	1	2		4	5	6	7	8		10	11				9							
19		25	Ashington	3-1	Cook(2), Matthewson	3245	1	2	3	4	5	6	7				11							9	8			
20		26	ASHINGTON	0-0		6328	1	2	3	4	5	6	7			10	11							9	8			
21		29	DARLINGTON	1-3	Hope	5402	1	2	3	4	8	6	7				11				10	9						5
22	Jan	1	Accrington Stanley	0-2		7039	1	2	3	8	5	6	7		9	10	11		4									
23		5	Southport	0-5		3040	1	2	3	8	5	6	7		9	10	11		4									
24		12	TRANMERE ROVERS	4-1	Matthewson(2), Kennedy(2)	3748	1	2	3		5	6	7	8	9	10	11		4									
25		19	ROCHDALE	5-2	Stevenson(3), Kennedy, Parker	3900	1	2	3		5	6	7	8	9	10	11		4									
26		26	New Brighton	0-1		3400	1	2	3		5	6	7	8	9	10	11		4									
27	Feb	2	WREXHAM	3-2	Reilly, Kennedy(2)	4255	1	2	3		5	6	7	8	9	10	11		4									
28		9	Chesterfield	2-3	Stevenson, Kennedy	3258	1	2	3		5	6	7	8	9	10	11		4									
29		23	Doncaster Rovers	1-2	Parker	7206		2			5	6	7	8	9	10	11		4				3				1	
30	Mar	2	HARTLEPOOLS UNITED	1-1	Stevenson	3728		2			5	6	7	8	9	10	11		4				3				1	
31		9	Carlisle United	0-5		7559		2			5	6	7	8	9				4		10					11	1	3
32		16	ROTHERHAM UNITED	10-1	Matthewson,Stevenson(2),Maycock(4),Kennedy,G Scott(2)	3134	1	2	3	4	5	6	7	8	10		11				9							
33		23	Wigan Borough	0-4		5223	1	2	3	4	5	6	7	8	10		11				9							
34		29	ACCRINGTON STANLEY	3-0	Maycock(2), G Scott	5940	1	2	3	4	5	6	7	8	10		11				9							
35		30	CREWE ALEXANDRA	3-0	Stevenson(2), G Scott	4091	1	2	3	4	5	6	7	8	10		11				9							
36	Apr	1	NELSON	3-2	Maycock(2), G Scott (pen)	4334	1	2	3	4	5	6	7	8	10		11				9							
37		6	Tranmere Rovers	0-4		4769	1	2	3	4	5	6	7	8	10		11				9							
38		13	STOCKPORT COUNTY	0-1		5597	1	2	3	4	5	6	7	8	10		11				9							
39		17	BARROW	2-2	Matthewson, Maycock	1468	1	2	3	4	5	6	7	8	10						9	11						
40		20	Halifax Town	2-0	Kennedy, Lowson (og)	3604	1	2			5	6	7	8	10						9	11	3					
41		27	LINCOLN CITY	1-0	Maycock	2542	1	2			5	6	7	8	10						9	11	3					
42	May	4	Bradford City	1-3	Kennedy	28850	1	2			5	6	7	8	10						9	11	3					
					Appearances		39	42	35	35	42	38	42	33	28	29	28	3	10	3	23	14	6	5	2	1	3	1
					Goals					2		3	13	16	11	10	6				18			2				

Additional Player: Murphy - Match 19/pos.10

2 Own Goals

F.A. Cup

		Date	Opponent	Score	Scorers	Att	Shevlin	Sinclair	Dunn	Hope	Davies	Reilly	Matthewson	Stevenson	Parker	Maycock	Talbot JH
R1	Nov	24	Accrington Stanley	1-2	Parker	5354	1	2	3	4	5	6	7	8	10	9	11

1928/29 Football League Division 3 (North)

		P	Home W	D	L	F	A	Away W	D	L	F	A	F	A	Pts
1	Bradford City	42	17	2	2	82	18	10	7	4	46	25	128	43	63
2	Stockport County	42	19	2	0	77	23	9	4	8	34	35	111	58	62
3	Wrexham	42	17	2	2	59	25	4	8	9	32	44	91	69	52
4	Wigan Borough	42	16	4	1	55	16	5	5	11	27	33	82	49	51
5	Doncaster Rovers	42	14	3	4	39	20	6	7	8	37	46	76	66	50
6	Lincoln City	42	15	3	3	58	18	6	3	12	33	49	91	67	48
7	Tranmere Rovers	42	15	3	3	55	21	7	0	14	24	56	79	77	47
8	Carlisle United	42	15	3	3	61	27	4	5	12	25	50	86	77	46
9	Crewe Alexandra	42	11	6	4	47	23	7	2	12	33	45	80	68	44
10	SOUTH SHIELDS	42	13	5	3	57	24	5	3	13	26	50	83	74	44
11	Chesterfield	42	13	2	6	46	28	5	3	13	25	49	71	77	41
12	Southport	42	13	5	3	52	27	3	3	15	23	58	75	85	40
13	Halifax Town	42	11	7	3	42	24	2	6	13	21	38	63	62	39
14	New Brighton	42	11	3	7	40	28	4	6	11	24	43	64	71	39
15	Nelson	42	14	1	6	48	28	3	4	14	29	62	77	90	39
16	Rotherham United	42	12	5	4	44	23	3	4	14	16	54	60	77	39
17	Rochdale	42	12	4	5	55	34	1	6	14	24	62	79	96	36
18	Accrington Stanley	42	11	5	5	42	22	2	3	16	26	60	68	82	34
19	Darlington	42	12	6	3	47	26	1	1	19	17	62	64	88	33
20	Barrow	42	7	6	8	42	37	3	2	16	22	56	64	93	28
21	Hartlepools United	42	9	4	8	35	38	1	2	18	24	74	59	112	26
22	Ashington	42	6	5	10	31	52	2	2	17	14	63	45	115	23

Average (Home) Attendance: 3300 (Lowest in Division 3[N])

#		Date	Opponent	Score	Scorers	Att	Carr	Sinclair	Turnbull	Davies	Nelson	Reilly	Matthewson	Kirk	Maycock	Kennedy	Talbot	Scott	Mustard	Littlewood	Taylor	Barkas	Charlton	Hope	Brown
1	Aug	31	Chesterfield	2-1	Maycock(2)	5404	1	2	3	4	5	6	7	8	9	10	11								
2	Sep	2	Doncaster Rovers	0-1		5824	1	2	3	4	5	6	7	8	9	10	11								
3		7	LINCOLN CITY	3-1	Maycock(2), Talbot	5071	1	2	3	4	5		7	8	9	10	11	6							
4		11	DONCASTER ROVERS	2-1	Kirk, Kennedy	4235	1	2	3	4	5		7	8	9	10	11	6							
5		14	TRANMERE ROVERS	1-5	Kirk	5452	1	2	3	4	5		7	8	9	10	11	6							
6		21	HALIFAX TOWN	1-0	Matthewson	2880	1	2	3	4	5	6	7	8	9	10	11								
7		28	Rotherham United	1-0	Kennedy	7054	1	2	3	4	5	6	7	8	9	10	11								
8	Oct	5	ROCHDALE	2-2	Maycock(2)	3876	1	2	3	4	5	6	7	8	9	10	11								
9		12	Wigan Borough	1-1	Littlewood	5170	1	2	3	4		6	7		9	10	11		8	5					
10		19	WREXHAM	1-1	Mustard	3572	1	2	3	4		6	7		9	10	11		8	5					
11		26	Barrow	3-1	Maycock, Kennedy(2)	4205	1	2	3	4	5	6		8	9	10	11		7						
12	Nov	2	PORT VALE	0-0		5984	1	2	3	4	5	6		8	9	10	11		7						
13		9	New Brighton	1-4	Kennedy	3112	1	2	3	4	5	6		8	9	10	11		7						
14		16	STOCKPORT COUNTY	2-3	Reilly, Kennedy	4971	1	2	3	4	5	6	7		9	10			8		11				
15		23	York City	2-2	Matthewson, Kennedy	3608	1	2	3	4	5		7		9	10		6	8		11				
16	Dec	7	Southport	1-2	Kirk	1702	1	2	3	4	5	6	7	9	8	10				11					
17		14	NELSON	2-1	Barkas(2)	3361	1	2	3	4	5	6	7	8	10					11		9			
18		21	Carlisle United	1-4	Barkas	5570	1	2	3	4	5	6	7	8	10					11		9			
19		25	Hartlepools United	1-2	Kennedy	3175		2	3	4	5	6	7		10					11		9			1
20		26	HARTLEPOOLS UNITED	3-5	Bowron (og), Taylor(2)	4118		2	3	4	5	6	7		10					11	9				1
21		28	CHESTERFIELD	3-1	Barkas, Kennedy, Taylor	2743	1	2	3	4	5	6			10					11	9	7			
22	Jan	1	Darlington	3-8	Matthewson, Barkas(2)	4573	1	2	3	4	5	6	7		10					11	9				
23		4	Lincoln City	2-2	Mustard, Barkas	5675	1	2	3		5				10				8	11	9	7	4		
24		11	CREWE ALEXANDRA	1-0	Barkas	2030	1	2	3		5				10				8	11	9	7	4		
25		18	Tranmere Rovers	0-3		4480	1	2	3		5				10				8	11	9	7	4		
26		25	Halifax Town	2-2	Barkas, Kennedy	4564	1	2	3		5	4	6		10				8	11	9	7			
27	Feb	1	ROTHERHAM UNITED	5-0	Barkas(2), Kennedy, Taylor(2)	1239	1	2	3		5	4			10			6	8	11	9	7			
28		8	Rochdale	0-2		3176	1	2	3		5	4	6		10				8	11	9	7			
29		15	WIGAN BOROUGH	2-2	Barkas, Taylor	2409	1	2	3		5	4	6		10				8	11	9	7			
30		22	Wrexham	3-1	Mustard, Kennedy, Taylor	3080	1	2	3		5	4	6	7	10				8	11	9				
31	Mar	1	BARROW	2-0	Matthewson, Barkas	2600	1	2	3		5	4	6	7	10				8	11	9				
32		8	Port Vale	0-3		9748	1	2	3		5	4	6	7	10				8	11	9				
33		15	NEW BRIGHTON	1-2	Mustard (pen)	2068	1	2	3		5	4	6		10				8	11	9	7			
34		22	Stockport County	0-2		6021	1	2	3		5	4	6		8	10					11	9	7		
35		29	YORK CITY	4-1	Barkas, Maycock(2), Talbot	2234	1	2	3		5	4	6	7	9	10	11				8				
36	Apr	5	Crewe Alexandra	2-2	Barkas, Kennedy	3638	1	2	3		5	4	6		9	10	11			7	8				
37		12	SOUTHPORT	4-0	Maycock(3), Talbot	1846	1	2	3		5	4	6		9	10	11		8					7	
38		18	DARLINGTON	3-3	Charlton, Maycock, Talbot	4777	1	2	3			4	6		9	10	11		8	5				7	
39		19	Nelson	1-0	Maycock	1553	1	3	2			6	4		9	8	7			5			10	11	
40		21	Accrington Stanley	2-1	Charlton, Talbot	2789	1	2	3			4	6		9	10	11		8	5				7	
41		26	CARLISLE UNITED	5-2	Charlton(3), Maycock(2)	2082	1	2	3			4	6		9	10	11		8	5				7	
42	May	3	ACCRINGTON STANLEY	2-2	Maycock, Kennedy	1752	1	2	3			4	6		9	10	11		8	5				7	
			Apps				40	42	42	37	37	25	12	24	42	21	5	31	7	18	21	16	3	2	
			Goals									1	4	3	17	14	5		4	1	15	5			

1 Own Goal

F.A. Cup

R		Date	Opponent	Score	Scorers	Att																			
R1	Nov	30	WREXHAM	2-4	Maycock, Mustard	5000	1	2	3	4	5	6	7	8	9	10			11						

1929/30 Football League Division 3 (North)

			Home				Away							
		P	W	D	L	F	A	W	D	L	F	A	F	A	Pts
1	Port Vale	42	17	2	2	64	18	13	5	3	39	19	103	37	67
2	Stockport County	42	15	3	3	67	20	13	4	4	39	24	106	44	63
3	Darlington	42	14	2	5	71	29	8	4	9	37	44	108	73	50
4	Chesterfield	42	18	1	2	53	15	4	5	12	23	41	76	56	50
5	Lincoln City	42	12	8	1	54	23	5	6	10	29	38	83	61	48
6	York City	42	11	7	3	43	20	4	9	8	34	44	77	64	46
7	SOUTH SHIELDS	42	11	6	4	49	32	7	4	10	28	42	77	74	46
8	Hartlepools United	42	13	4	4	50	24	4	7	10	31	50	81	74	45
9	Southport	42	11	5	5	49	31	4	8	9	32	43	81	74	43
10	Rochdale	42	14	3	4	57	30	4	4	13	32	61	89	91	43
11	Crewe Alexandra	42	12	5	4	55	28	5	3	13	27	43	82	71	42
12	Tranmere Rovers	42	12	4	5	57	35	4	5	12	26	51	83	86	41
13	New Brighton	42	13	4	4	48	22	3	4	14	21	57	69	79	40
14	Doncaster Rovers	42	13	5	3	39	22	2	4	15	23	47	62	69	39
15	Carlisle United	42	13	4	4	63	34	3	3	15	27	67	90	101	39
16	Accrington Stanley	42	11	4	6	55	30	3	5	13	29	51	84	81	37
17	Wrexham	42	10	5	6	42	28	3	3	15	25	60	67	88	34
18	Wigan Borough	42	12	4	5	44	26	1	3	17	16	62	60	88	33
19	Nelson	42	9	4	8	31	25	4	3	14	20	55	51	80	33
20	Rotherham United	42	9	4	8	46	40	2	4	15	21	73	67	113	30
21	Halifax Town	42	7	7	7	27	26	3	1	17	17	53	44	79	28
22	Barrow	42	9	4	8	31	28	2	1	18	10	70	41	98	27

THE HORSLEY HILL STADIUM STORY

The home ground of South Shields Football Club during their Football League career was also used at various times for greyhound racing and boxing but originally it had been the home of South Shields Rugby Union Club who first played matches there in September 1900. Their secretary at this time was none other than the youthful Jack Tinn.

Five years earlier several clubs in Yorkshire and Lancashire had broken away from the Rugby Union over the issue of payments to compensate players for loss of earnings and had founded the Northern Union (later to be known as the Rugby League). Many clubs of varying sizes had converted but the North East's Rugby Union clubs had been unaffected by this acrimonious split. South Shields, however, predicted that if they took the plunge they would be followed by a number of others. Accordingly they con-verted to the new code in 1901 and after a season of playing friendly matches they were elected into the second division. No other North Eastern club followed their example and South Shields found themselves out on a limb geographically with no opponents nearer than York.

The short history of Northern Union at Horsley Hill bears an uncanny resemblance to that of the soccer club several years later. Jack Tinn set off on his travels to sign experienced players from Barrow, Wigan and Hull as well as a famous Rugby Union International named Jowett from Hartlepool Rovers. The division South Shields played in had a decidedly Third Division (North) look to it with visits to Barrow, Rochdale, Stockport and Birkenhead. The three last named clubs entertained South Shields at the home grounds of Rochdale FC, Stockport County and Tranmere Rovers while another opponent, Manningham, played their home games at Valley Parade before the club converted to soccer and evolved into Bradford City FC.

Some famous Rugby League names visited South Shields including Warrington, Wakefield Trinity and Castleford (whom South Shields beat 33-0) but other opponents were fellow " fly by night" clubs such as Normanton, Millom and Brighouse. The Shields Daily Gazette would not pay for a reporter to travel to away matches relying instead on letters from correspondents in the towns concerned. Saturday matches were reported in the following Tuesday's columns which offered warm congratulations on the few victories and commiserations for the occasional heavy defeat.

The venture was doomed from the start. Finishing 14th out of 18 in the first season and with no sign of any other North Eastern Rugby Union club following their example the club began the 1903-4 season with the players agreeing to forego arrears of payment. Crowds rarely reached a thousand and travelling expenses took their inevitable toll. When the club was summonsed for non-payment of a Manchester hotel bill early in 1904 the announcement that it was on the point of folding came as no surprise. The club ended their second and last League season in 15th position out of 17.

After the demise of the Rugby club the Horsley Hill ground does not seem to have been used until the soccer club took it over shortly before joining the North Eastern League in 1908.

In the early years facilities seem to have been rather basic. Years later an old player remembered a rat from an adjoining field finding its way into the home dressing room just before a match with Sunderland Reserves. This unwelcome visitor so upset South Shields player Mark Randall that he ran out onto the pitch in a state of near nakedness to the delight of that season's largest crowd.

In 1912 the club began to seriously contemplate applying for Football League membership and a new stand was built in the summer of that year. The following year the club purchased a further stand and a pavilion second-hand when a racecourse at nearby Boldon was taken over by a coal company. After the War the prospectus for the successful Football League application boasted of £2000 having been spent on improving the pitch and providing dressing room and stand accommodation.

Now knowing what the state of the Horsley Hill pitch was like during the Football League days an obvious question presents itself; what on earth must it have been like before? However, the claim of offering covered accommodation for 5000 was something to be proud of and was something which larger and richer clubs could not equal. Further work was being done with much tipping and banking as the club entered the League and a cover over the Sea End was completed in March 1920.

One would dearly love to know what became of " *the collection of photographic souvenirs which hang in the pavilion at Horsley Hill* " (Shields Football Gazette, 9 January 1926) and there is even a reference to a film of a pre-First World War South Shields match being shown at a local cinema in 1936. This was the year in which the new South Shields club was formed, largely as a result of a campaign by the Shields Gazette. That club joined the North Eastern League and commanded large crowds at Horsley Hill before and after the Second World War.

After the Football League club moved to Gateshead the Horsley Hill ground became a greyhound stadium. These dissimilar sports have shared grounds in many towns, bringing in additional revenue to the football club, but the arrangement has not always been a happy one with the football authorities taking rather a dim view. In the late Forties, visiting teams complained that the metal equipment surrounding the much reduced pitch was endangering players and in November 1949 the club moved to a new location at Simonside although occasional matches were still played at Horsley Hill later that season.

A light-hearted "nostalgia" match was played at Horsley Hill each Good Friday from 1949 to 1955. This was organised by George Lillycrop in aid of local charities and often drew crowds bordering on five figures. Religious people with qualms about football being played on that day could console themselves that the spirit of forgiveness was manifested in 1950 with George Camsell cheerfully playing in the same side as his old tormentor Cyril Hunter. Other old South Shields players in those matches included Warney Cresswell, Alan Taylor, Tommy Charlton and George Lillycrop himself whilst other old stars such as Hughie Gallacher sometimes put in an appearance.

Press photographs of various minor games played at Horsley Hill in the Fifties show the ground to be little changed from Football League days but the greyhound stadium did not prosper for very much longer. In February 1966 greyhound racing's regulatory body announced that as a result of a recent inspection racing at Horsley Hill was to cease forthwith.

Elsewhere in the town the senior South Shields club was putting in some fair performances in the F.A.Cup defeating the occasional League club such as Chesterfield, Crewe Alexandra and Oldham Athletic, all of whom had previous experience of returning home from South Shields empty-handed. In 1970 the club reached the Third Round losing to Queens Park Rangers at Loftus Road just as their Second Division predecessors had done in 1923.

In the Fifties and Sixties the club applied for membership of the Football League (some people never learn) but eventually they went the way of their Northern Rugby Union and Football League forebears, literally in the latter case.

In 1974 they moved to Gateshead (yes, there was a Football League club once there!).

Recently the author of this book walked round the rather pleasant housing estate between Horsley Hill Road and St. Vincent Street noting down the name of roads named after golf courses (Birkdale, Muirfield, Gleneagles). Two boys paused from kicking a football and enquired what I was about. I wondered if they knew that Manchester United once lost a bad tempered match on that very spot or that Chelsea had been beaten 5-1 here in a hurricane. No, they wouldn't have believed it.

Time goes by and the past is lost forever. Or is it? Whilst diligently pursuing my researches in a nearby hostelry (The Fountain) a gentleman told me how he was walking home late one night in the 1960's when he noticed a man standing in the vicinity of the gates of the old football ground. Continuing to walk down that road my informant was astonished to find that the man had seemingly vanished into thin air and the incident had baffled him ever since.

Who can this spectre have been? Some aggrieved centre-forward looking for Cyril Hunter perhaps? Or the ghost of a 1919 referee forced to wander the earth forever as punishment for failing to arrive at Horsley Hill on time? Or his colleague who baffled the South Shields magistrate in 1925 returning to the terraces to seek further evidence to justify his citizen's arrest? The possibilities are endless.

Horsley Hill, taken in 1932 after South Shields had departed.
Work is underway in creating a Greyhound Stadium.